you're going to be okay

you're going to be okay

16 Lessons on Healing after Trauma

Madeline Popelka

HAY HOUSE

Carlsbad, California • New York City
London • Sydney • New Delhi

Published in the United Kingdom by:
Hay House UK Ltd, The Sixth Floor, Watson House,
54 Baker Street, London W1U 7BU
Tel: +44 (0)20 3927 7290; Fax: +44 (0)20 3927 7291; www.hayhouse.co.uk

Published in the United States of America by:
Hay House Inc., PO Box 5100, Carlsbad, CA 92018-5100
Tel: (1) 760 431 7695 or (800) 654 5126
Fax: (1) 760 431 6948 or (800) 650 5115; www.hayhouse.com

Published in Australia by:
Hay House Australia Ltd, 18/36 Ralph St, Alexandria NSW 2015
Tel: (61) 2 9669 4299; Fax: (61) 2 9669 4144; www.hayhouse.com.au

Published in India by:
Hay House Publishers India, Muskaan Complex, Plot No.3, B-2,
Vasant Kunj, New Delhi 110 070
Tel: (91) 11 4176 1620; Fax: (91) 11 4176 1630; www.hayhouse.co.in

Project editor: Melody Guy
Cover design: Julie Davison
Interior design: Bryn Starr Best

A catalogue record for this book is available from the British Library.

Tradepaper ISBN: 978-1-83782-059-7
Hardback ISBN: 978-1-4019-6824-3
E-book ISBN: 978-1-4019-6825-0
Audiobook ISBN: 978-1-4019-6826-7

Printed and bound by CPI Group (UK) Ltd, Croydon CR0 4YY

To anyone who is hurting and struggling to find their way.
You are not alone.

contents

introduction

I used to believe that healing was effortless, and something that just happened to you. I assumed that, like a cut, my internal wounds would naturally heal with time if I didn't do anything to irritate or infect them. I thought that if I just forgot about what I went through, my pain would fade away.

If only healing were that easy.

I've had a few traumatic experiences over the course of my life. While each one shook me to my core, I never recognized that what I'd been through was *traumatic*. Because I was never harmed physically, I was always able to convince myself that what I went through wasn't a big deal. But I was wrong.

As the daughter of a refugee with a traumatic past, I experienced the effects of unhealed trauma as a young girl. My mother loved me and always wanted to provide me with opportunities she'd never had. But when I'd pushed her buttons, she'd explode, chasing me around the house and threatening to beat me with a broom. While she never struck me, I was terrified, and I'd spend hours hiding in my closet crying. I always thought that it was my fault. I thought that if I didn't talk back, if I were as smart as my older sister, or if I were just a better person, I wouldn't have made her do that to me. These memories were too painful to hold, so I buried them and didn't look back.

When I was 26, on my way to the farmers' market one morning, I had to run for my life when a man began chasing after me. I breathlessly screamed for help, hoping someone would hear me, but there wasn't anyone around. In survival mode, I jumped in front of the first car I saw—I would have rather been hit by a car than suffer an attack. Getting the driver's attention was enough to scare my pursuer off, and I ended up walking away untouched. I told myself, *Get over it. It wasn't that bad,* and I forced myself to move on.

Then, 18 months later, I witnessed my friend running out of a bathroom with tears streaming down her face after being drugged and sexually assaulted by a man I knew. What started out as an enjoyable evening of catching up over wine turned into a nightmare that I couldn't forgive myself for. I felt guilty for not being able to stop it from happening, and I was afraid: being so close to what happened that night made me feel like it could have just as easily happened to me. And because a stranger had invited himself to put his hands in my shorts in college, and because I was sexually harassed by a work colleague when I was 22, I felt like something similar *would* happen to me. Yet because it was my friend who suffered the assault, and not me, I pushed my fears aside.

Soon I became a person who was terrified of the world. I *never* felt safe, even in my own home. Every time I heard an unexpected noise, like a knock on the front door, my heart would race. I had visions of myself opening the door and getting beaten, kidnapped, or raped. I started to experience anxiety daily, and a few mornings each week, I'd wake up in sweat-drenched sheets in a panic after having a nightmare. Little by little, these symptoms intensified, and eventually, they made it impossible to work, sleep, or hold conversations with my partner. I felt like I was losing my mind, and at the time, I didn't have a clue why. But I was determined to find out.

I re-evaluated every aspect of my life. I first thought that one of my clients who never paid me on time might be responsible for making me anxious, so I stopped working with that company. I thought that I might have been spending too much time on social media, so I implemented a "no social media after 7:30 P.M." rule (probably for the best). I took a mini vacation to a tiny town in wine country and stayed in a B&B with no technology—just board games, books, and fire pits. I thought my diet wasn't nutritious enough, so I got back on my plant-based regimen and cut back on alcohol. I was living the healthiest, most relaxing life I knew how to live, but the anxiety and panic were still there. I was desperate to find some relief; I just wanted to be able to feel "normal" again. I finally realized that I needed help from a professional, so I sought treatment from a psychologist, which led to a diagnosis of posttraumatic stress disorder (PTSD).

As I worked to manage my PTSD symptoms in therapy, I continued to struggle with nightmares, anxiety, and depression. Healing doesn't happen overnight—unfortunately, your therapist can't magically heal your wounds for you. Nightmares and panic attacks made my first year of marriage so much more challenging and less fun than I wished. When I had vivid dreams and intrusive thoughts about a rapist coming to attack me, I didn't want to be touched or anywhere near men. Severe anxiety made it impossible to function day-to-day, and when depression came, I wanted to disappear. I felt worthless, like I was damaged and had no purpose in life. I asked myself, *Why me? Why did I have to go through trauma? Why can't I be "normal"?*

I let some relationships fall apart because I didn't want people in my life to see me struggling. When I could, I avoided people, making excuses for not meeting up for lunch, or going to events. Whenever I had to see people for work or social gatherings, I scraped up all the energy I could to put on a show, pretending to be cheerful and confident. But the moment I'd get back home (or the second I made it into my car), I'd burst into tears and cry, sometimes for hours. It was painful to hide what I was going through, but telling people wasn't an option: I thought it would be the worst thing if they ever found out. I was ashamed.

After nearly a year of treatment and being intentional with my healing, I noticed my progress. My anxiety softened, nightmares and panic attacks became rare, and I started retrieving the confidence I had lost while suffering. I realized that what happened to me wasn't my fault—that trauma cannot be prevented—and that struggling with PTSD wasn't a weakness, but something that had helped me grow. I started seeing the positives woven within my healing journey, and I realized I had become a better person: more empathetic, compassionate, insightful, and emotionally intelligent. I decided to embrace my new life as a trauma survivor, including the painful moments that come along with it, which ultimately led me to find as much joy as I ever remembered having. For the first time in my life, I experienced self-love.

Even when my PTSD symptoms faded away, my healing journey wasn't over. Having experienced trauma at a young age damaged my self-esteem, and since then, dozens of experiences—from being cheated on to being denied a promotion that I was promised—have reinforced this idea that I wasn't enough, didn't matter, and that there was something wrong with me. Healing from trauma isn't just making peace with major events that happened: it also involves untangling deep-seated, inaccurate beliefs that we hold as a result of that trauma. Part of healing is letting go of these beliefs and then learning to accept ourselves as imperfect human beings.

I am still healing, and I'm more than okay with it. While healing can be excruciatingly painful, I've learned to cherish the journey. Getting to know yourself better can be incredibly fulfilling. Learning to let others see your pain can help create loving and supportive relationships. Shedding layers of shame often helps you reconnect with joy. Healing brings so many gifts, and while I am not grateful for having experienced trauma, I am grateful that healing has helped me grow into a person I'm proud of.

Nobody ever showed me how to tend to my emotional wounds. If anything, my parents, teachers, and societal mores taught me to suppress my feelings and "move on." I tried that, and it only caused more pain; once, it even led to a suicide attempt. When I was suffering, I didn't think that healing was possible. I thought that I was broken and that I'd just have to get used to living with fear and piercing shame. I gave up on myself once, but I'm so glad I haven't again. Healing is possible, friends.

Since I began sharing my story about healing from trauma, many survivors have asked me, "How do I heal?" Now that I've been on this journey for four years, I've realized that healing isn't something that can be easily taught. There is no single way to heal; healing from trauma is a deeply personal journey. Each traumatic experience carries its own complexities, and we're all unique individuals with different personalities and preferences. There's an infinite number of paths one could take to heal, and part of healing is figuring out what combinations of activities are best for you, whether that includes therapy, mindfulness, spirituality, or creativity. Our needs can also change; I've been a hundred different versions of myself since I've started healing, and my needs at the beginning of my journey are not the same as my needs now. As humans, we continuously evolve, and our healing requirements also evolve as we come across new obstacles and opportunities along the way.

Because I don't know what's best for *your* healing, I'm not going to tell you the specific activities and coping techniques you should incorporate in your life, but I will help you figure it out. I'll guide you through the internal steps I took to begin my own healing journey, and what I did to continue promoting that healing. I'm sharing the 16 key lessons that I wish I learned sooner, and the insights I gained that shifted my perspective and reduced my shame, with the hopes that they will do the same for you. I'm sharing what I needed to hear when I didn't get the encouragement I wanted from my friends, family, or therapist. I'm sharing the thoughts that brought me comfort and peace when I was feeling isolated, and I hope that by sharing my story, you feel less alone and are inspired to take your healing into your own hands.

Healing looks different for everyone, so please don't compare my journey (or anyone else's) to yours. My story is one of millions, and my experience doesn't mirror the experience of every trauma survivor out there. Each one of us faces unique challenges, and not everyone has access to the same resources and opportunities. Throughout my healing journey, I've had access to mental health care. I live in an environment where I feel safe. I have a supportive partner and financial stability. I've had so many advantages on this journey, and I know not everyone is in the same position. While hard work and dedication makes healing possible, it isn't the only thing that helped get me to where I am today. If your healing journey doesn't look like mine, that doesn't mean you're doing it wrong. Your healing doesn't have to look a certain way for it to be valid.

As I share my stories of trauma and healing throughout this book, it will lead you to think about your own experiences. While they will provide comfort and validation, these stories may also bring up some unpleasant feelings. If at any point you feel like this book is too much to handle, it's okay to step away for a few days, or however long you need, and pick it back up when you're ready.

I know things may be really painful right now. Surviving a traumatic experience is devastating, and it can turn your world upside down. While I wish you didn't have to go through what you did, I'm proud of you for being here, and for showing up for yourself: it takes courage to face your past. Picking up this book demonstrates a commitment to your journey, and while it will be messy and uncomfortable and challenging every step of the way, I can already tell you'll have the strength to make it.

It may not feel like it at this moment, but I promise you're going to be okay.

CHAPTER 1

you can't erase
your past

After every traumatic experience I went through, I told myself, *I just want to forget about it and move on.* I wanted to forget because looking back on my traumas made me feel anxious and afraid. I wanted to forget because I didn't think that what I went through was a big deal and that I should just let it go. I wanted to forget because I was ashamed of my past, and no longer wanted it to be a part of me. I wanted to forget because I never wanted to go through those experiences in the first place, and the memories and feelings were too painful to hold.

I thought that forgetting was how I could release the pain and discomfort my traumas created. At the time, all I wanted to do was move through life unaffected by my past, and I believed that forgetting about what happened was the only way to get there. I was focused on building a better future, so I discarded the memories and feelings that I didn't want to take with me.

When I was 26, I thought I finally had life figured out. I had just quit my corporate job where I felt undervalued and underpaid, and started a consulting business, doing work I was passionate about. I fell in love for the first time with my partner, Adam, and we shared a cozy 600-square-foot apartment. I was enjoying city life in San Francisco: going out to nice restaurants, having picnics with breathtaking views of the Golden Gate Bridge, and dancing at cocktail bars with my friends. I was the happiest I had ever been, and I wasn't going to let anything ruin it.

My friend Kendall and I had a Saturday morning ritual of going to the farmers' market at the Ferry Building together each week. The farmers' market was our favorite place in the city, with bounties of fresh fruit, drool-worthy pastries, and the prettiest flowers that we couldn't wait to set on our dining tables. We'd walk there with cappuccinos in hand, admiring the charming Beaux-Arts apartments with magenta bougainvillea crawling up the garages and balconies. But one Saturday in late November, I was planning to escape the fog that often blankets the city and drive up to Napa to enjoy sunshine, wine-tasting, and cheese-eating with friends. Because my schedule didn't align with Kendall's, I decided to make the farmers' market trip by myself.

When I walked to the Ferry Building that morning, I wasn't alone. I started to hear footsteps behind me once I reached the Financial District; they sounded like block heels clapping on the concrete. At first, I thought that it was just someone trying to pass me on the sidewalk, so I slowed down so they could take the lead, and when they didn't, I sped up to see if they'd start trailing behind. No matter how quickly or slowly I took my strides, the person followed closely. At one point, they were so close that I could see men's dress shoes and tan skinny jeans clinging tightly to a pair of ankles in my peripheral vision. My heart raced as I began to worry that I was being followed; there wasn't another human, other than the two of us, in sight.

While the Financial District is alive on workdays with people rushing to their 9-to-5 jobs, it's a ghost town at 7:30 A.M. on a Saturday. Still, I told myself, *I'm just being paranoid*, and kept walking, hoping he'd start falling behind.

After I reached the end of the block, I still heard the footsteps, so I tried one last test before freaking out: I bolted to the left side of the sidewalk into an ATM nook, the one that Kendall and I usually stopped at to withdraw cash for the market. Standing with my back to the street, I listened for his footsteps—this was his chance to walk past me. I thought I heard footfalls in the distance and figured he'd continue down the street. But I had to double-check, so I turned my head to look over my right shoulder.

My stomach dropped. A man was standing about six feet behind me, glaring at me. I knew he was after me, so I didn't even think about it—I just ran. And he came after me.

Heart pounding, I raced down the sidewalk, scanning for anyone who could help me. Even though there wasn't anybody around, I thought someone might be able to hear me, so I started to scream, "HELP! HELP!" in a terrified voice that I didn't even recognize. I looked over my shoulder and saw he was trailing only a couple of feet behind me.

After sprinting down two blocks that felt like miles, I was winded and didn't know if I could go on. I didn't have any breath left to run or scream anymore, and he was almost close enough to reach his arm out and grab me. I thought, *This is it. He's going to get me,* and prepared myself for the worst. But then, I looked over my right shoulder and saw a car—a taxi—driving down the street, and I jumped off the sidewalk and into the street to run toward it.

The taxi stopped, and I ran to the driver's window. The man stopped in front of the hood of the car. I banged on the window, screaming, "HELP! He's following me!" The driver rolled down the window and said something—what it was, I can't remember. I was concentrating on my pursuer, who immediately started backing away from the taxi, hands raised. "What are you talking about?" he said in a condescending tone. Then he walked away.

Even though he was heading off in a different direction, I didn't feel safe. *He could turn around and chase me again*, I thought. I was shaking from head to toe, and my heart was pounding so hard that I thought I'd have a heart attack. I wanted to cry but couldn't—the terror somehow blocked my tears. I ran the rest of the way to the farmers' market, looking over my shoulder every couple of seconds to make sure he didn't sneak up behind me again.

Even when I reached the Ferry Building—a place where I always felt safe—I couldn't shake the sense that I was in danger. It felt like the man was still following me, so I ended up spending more time looking behind me than at the fruit I was buying. I was more clumsy than usual, dropping bags and dollars on the ground. I bumped into a table of Early Girl tomatoes, causing them to roll onto the ground, ruining the perfect display. Whenever someone came up behind me, I jumped in the air and gasped, then walked away. Everyone and everything was overwhelming to me, so I called a Lyft and got a ride home.

When I texted Kendall and told her what had happened, she couldn't believe it. Neither could Adam when I told him. At one point, he asked, "Are you sure this guy really exists?" As if I was crazy.

I wasn't crazy—he was real. But I wasn't going to let him ruin my day or the perfect life I was creating. So, once we got in the car to head up to Napa, I pretended like it never happened and tried my best to abandon my memories.

Unhealed trauma will always find a way to remind you of what you went through.

In the months following that experience, no matter how hard I tried to ignore it, and no matter how many times I told myself, *Get over it,* I couldn't shake my fear. Desperate to make myself feel better, I did everything in my power to push those thoughts away. I distracted myself with work, using my new business as an excuse to always be busy, and I truly was, sending off e-mails at 5:00 A.M. and working until Adam came home from work to entertain me. I'd make happy hour plans with friends four days a week, keeping myself preoccupied by gossiping over drinks. I couldn't be still—I always had to be doing something. In the rare moment I'd let myself relax, my mind would start spinning with terrifying thoughts about men coming to attack me, and when the thoughts came, I'd avoid them by telling myself, "Okay, let's not go there. Focus!"

I wasn't just avoiding the thoughts. I used to walk *everywhere*, but didn't feel safe walking anywhere anymore, so I started getting more rides. I stopped working from the neighborhood coffee shop and only worked at home, just to avoid the four-block walk there and back. I didn't even leave my apartment if I peeked out my window and saw a questionable character of any kind outside my building; I would wait to see which direction the person was heading before leaving. Being chased had shaken me, and I avoided everything that had to do with it to protect myself.

Soon, I didn't feel safe in San Francisco anymore—even in my own apartment. The city had lost its charm, so Adam and I moved to the suburbs in the East Bay Hills two and a half years after the chasing incident. Our new home was so peaceful compared to the city. We heard birds singing during the day and crickets chirping at night, instead of car horns and obnoxious bros yelling as they walked home from the bars. A mama deer and her two fawns frequently visited our backyard, eating the ivy growing over our retaining wall and resting in the shady spot under our olive tree. I felt like Snow White, baking pies, surrounded by all my animal friends.

I knew I was safe, but I still didn't feel safe. Maybe it was *too quiet* in the hills. When I walked in the neighborhood alone, I often wondered, *If I had to scream for help, would anyone hear me?* When fall came, people would spook me by crunching on leaves as they walked behind me. I always stepped to the side and let everyone pass, as my anxiety spiked whenever I sensed someone behind me.

Even though we were in a quieter environment, I started experiencing sleep issues after we moved. I'd wake up to Adam in the middle of the night petting my arm and shoulder, saying, "It's okay, it's okay." In the morning, he'd tell me, "You were breathing really hard last night in your sleep," or "You were panting and crying," or "You were yelling for help." I could never remember my dreams, but

I'd wake up exhausted in sweat-drenched sheets as if I'd just run a marathon.

One morning, I woke up at 3:00 A.M. with my heart racing. I tried to fall back asleep, but my anxiety was so intense that I couldn't focus on anything other than the discomfort I felt in my chest. Once the sun rose, I tried to shake it off by going to a Pilates class, but immediately afterward, as I was walking to my car, fear jolted through me as I heard footsteps behind me. My entire body started shaking, and I couldn't find enough air to breathe. I thought to myself, *Oh my god, what is happening? Am I going to die?! I'M CRAZY.*

This first panic attack was rapidly followed by two more. My mind and body allowed me to push the trauma away for three years and two months until it said, *No more.*

66

You can't shove your past into the back of your closet to collect dust and expect to heal.

99

Trying to forget was a temporary coping strategy. Instead of healing my emotional wounds, I just worked around them, avoiding anything that reminded me of my trauma so that the pain wouldn't feel so intense. It didn't help me heal, but it allowed me to continue on with life, still hurt. Ignoring what happened didn't change what I went through. It didn't change the fact that I ran for my life out of fear that I would be attacked that day. My avoidance didn't take my fears away—if anything, it intensified them. Avoidance didn't take my pain away, but it did delay my healing process. Emotional wounds still exist even if we pretend they're not there.

The thing is, no matter how hard we may try, it's almost impossible to forget our traumas. The adrenaline that rushes through our bodies during traumatic events also helps engrave these experiences in our minds (Van der Kolk, *The Body Keeps the Score*, 2015). I'll never forget the sound of those footsteps behind me or the fear I felt as I ran for my life. For years, I tried my best to push the terrifying memories away, but unavoidable external cues, like hearing footsteps, would remind me of my trauma. And when these reminders came around, I felt like I was in danger, and would start to panic.

I thought I was protecting myself and the perfect life I was creating, but my avoidance ultimately caused more pain. When I buried my fears, they grew stronger below the surface, soon to explode in a series of panic attacks that made it impossible to work, sleep, or care for myself or others. It wasn't until I started processing my trauma head-on that I began to find relief from my panic attacks, severe anxiety, and nightmares. I didn't begin healing until I developed awareness around my wound and told myself, *I'm going to work through this.*

I used to think that healing was about forgetting what happened and never looking back. Now, I realize that healing requires sitting with what happened and learning to feel safe again, despite terrifying past experiences. I've learned that healing is a process of changing my relationship with what happened, and making peace with it, so that when I look back on the experience, I'm no longer overwhelmed by fear, judgment, and shame. My fear controlled me, fueling my avoidance. Healing has involved learning to see things, and myself, with more clarity, so that fear no longer takes the driver's seat.

Trauma is unpredictable, and it arrives at inconvenient times. We'll always be able to find reasons not to address our traumatic experiences, and no time will ever feel like the "right" time to deal with it, but trauma isn't going to disappear just because we don't give it our attention.

Start by acknowledging that what you went through was traumatic: this is where healing begins. Sometimes we avoid labeling our experiences as "trauma" because we don't think that what we went through was "that bad," and we don't want to be seen as weak. Sometimes it's because we think we're to blame for what happened, or because we're ashamed. Sometimes it's because it's painful to admit that those we care for harmed us. But we can't heal unless we're honest with ourselves about how our experiences impacted us.

I'm not going to lie to you: confronting your trauma can be brutal. Stepping into your darkness can be terrifying, stressful, and bring out a mess of unwanted emotions. Things may even feel like they're getting worse before they get better. But as you begin unpacking your trauma and sifting through the uncomfortable thoughts and feelings that come along with it, little by little, your fears won't feel as threatening, your pain won't feel as heavy, and you'll start to find relief.

You may not be able to erase your past, but you have the power to free yourself from it. Validate your trauma and let the healing journey begin.

CHAPTER 2

trauma doesn't have an expiration date

Most of us have grown up with the idea that time heals all wounds—that as the hours, days, and years pass by, pain will soften, and things will get better. Though this can be true for some experiences, as I discovered while healing from heartbreak after being cheated on, with deeper psychological wounds, the memories of unhealed trauma are often just as painful decades later.

On an unseasonably warm Saturday in late November, Adam and I were enjoying a relaxing afternoon, lounging around in our backyard. The sun warmed my limbs as I sipped sparkling water and dove into the novel I was hoping to finish before the weekend ended. Once the sun began to set, goose bumps appeared on my forearms. I told Adam, "It's getting cold. Let's put the furniture away."

Our new patio furniture had just arrived, including a sectional couch with white cushions. Although we knew it would eventually transform into a beige couch, we did our best to protect it from the birds, trees, and shrubs with purple berries.

I dusted off the cushions as Adam retrieved the covers. When I heard Adam carrying the 10-foot-long tarps behind me, I said, "Hold on a second," as I continued brushing away dirt and specks of redwood needles. The next thing I knew, the light disappeared, and I was between the couch and the tarp. I felt trapped, like I was suffocating. I screamed, "Wait!"

My heart raced as I threw the tarp off me. Panting, I asked him, "Why did you cover me?" I could hear my voice rising as the words left my lips.

"Jeez, I didn't!" With pinched eyebrows, he gave me the *what are you talking about* look.

"Yes, you did!" I snapped back. "Why did you cover me when I asked you to hold on? Why didn't you wait?"

Annoyed, he yelled, "It was a mistake!" as he threw his head back toward the sky. Then he looked back at me and continued. "Can you just *calm down*?"

One of the most unhelpful things someone could tell me when I'm angry or upset is "calm down." I've always found it dismissive and passive-aggressive, sending the message that I don't have a right or a valid reason to feel the way I do.

My blood boiled as I yelled, "I told you, I *hate* when you tell me that."

His voice softened. "I'm sorry, okay? I didn't hear you. I didn't mean to do it."

I was heated, and I didn't want to be anywhere near him. I had learned earlier in our relationship that it's better if I dump my anger into my journal instead of saying something I might regret. So I stormed into the house, grabbed my notebook, and ran into our bedroom, slamming the door behind me.

As I started to write about what had just happened, I quickly realized that my anger wasn't about the tarp or Adam—I knew it was a mistake. I knew he wouldn't purposefully cover me like that. I knew that what happened wasn't a big deal, but it *felt* like a big deal. I was triggered.

I asked myself, *Why did being covered like that trigger me?* I laid down on my bed, searching myself for a memory of a time when being in an enclosed space scared me. I thought about how my sister and her friend trapped me in a closet during a sleepover for a few seconds, but I knew that wasn't it. After about five minutes of staring at the ceiling, a vision appeared. I saw myself as a terrified young girl—eight or nine years old—balled up in the corner of my bedroom closet, squeezing my knees into my chest, with clothes draped over my head and body.

My heart raced as I questioned the accuracy of my memory. I thought, *Did that really happen?* Immediately I burst into tears, crying uncontrollably. Other memories flooded in—ones that I'd been burying for decades because they were too painful to hold. While there were holes in so many of them, I *knew* it was true. I could feel it.

Time doesn't make emotional pain disappear.

Growing up, when I did something that made my mom angry, like talk back, she'd furiously rush to the corner of the kitchen where she kept the broom. She wouldn't say anything at first, but I knew what the broom meant, so when she did this, I'd run up the stairs as fast as I could. She'd come after me yelling, "WHAT DID YOU SAY?" My sisters and I didn't have locks on our doors, so once I'd get to my room, I'd hide in my closet or under my bed. If I had a big enough head start, I'd sometimes sneak into my parents' room and hide in their closet under my dad's suits. As I got older and my legs got longer, I was able to keep my bedroom door shut—and my mom out—by sitting with my back to the door with my feet pressed against my dresser in front of me.

My mom always knew where I was hiding, but she never pulled me out from the closet or from under the bed to strike me as her parents had struck her as a girl. In Vietnam, corporal punishment was the norm, and she endured physical pain daily. Yet she knew that in America, it wasn't an acceptable form of discipline. Instead, she would smack the broom against a door, the floor, a bedframe, or the banister, to scare me into behaving better. And it worked—I was terrified.

After she did this, I'd cry in my hiding place, thinking about what I did to deserve it. I knew that if I hadn't talked back, I wouldn't have made her so angry. I thought that I wasn't worthy of her love because I wasn't a straight-A student like my older sister and wasn't as adorable and innocent as my baby sister. I thought that I was born a bad kid, and that I was unlovable. I convinced myself that I deserved to be treated like that to make sense of it all. I was hurt, and I didn't know what else to do other than to push my feelings away and act like it had never happened.

Even though this happened decades earlier, starting around when I was seven years old, the pain felt just as intense when I started retrieving these memories in my late twenties. When a trigger came that sparked a memory of my mother chasing after me with a broom, I'd cry just as hard as I did when I was hiding from her in my closet. As I recalled how I felt as a child, like I was never loved and never could be loved, the thoughts quickly spiraled into depression. Time never healed these wounds. Time alone cannot heal—it's not magic.

If you're waiting for time to heal you, you'll be waiting forever.

Time didn't make my pain disappear. If anything, time helped me become more comfortable living with the pain. Throughout my childhood and adolescence, I found ways to cope. I found comfort in food and would eat everything in the pantry until I made myself sick. When I was in middle school, I'd cut myself in the bathtub. I'd cry in the pink-tinted bathwater, asking myself, *Why do I have to be me? Why couldn't I have been born someone else?* In high school, I started finding relief from my negative self-talk by smoking weed, numbing my emotions. This continued into college, where I began getting blackout drunk with friends five days a week. I hooked up with people that I barely knew each week because I thought I was undesirable, and I wanted to be wanted. I was reckless because I felt like I didn't have anything to lose—if anything ended my life, that would've been fine with me. Time went on, and I continued moving through life hurt, while pretending that I was fine.

I didn't begin healing from my childhood trauma until I acknowledged what had happened and how it affected me. (And because the person who harmed me is someone I love and care for, and someone who I know loves and cares for me, this wasn't an easy task.) Time didn't change the facts of what took place back then. Time didn't change what my mom did to me, or how it made me feel. As a 30-year-old, I'd beat myself up for still feeling hurt from what I went through as a kid. I'd think, *Shouldn't I be over this by now?* And as the flashbacks kept coming in, I felt ashamed and overwhelmed with sadness because I *still* wasn't over it.

While time offers no magic fix, I will say that it can be helpful on our healing journeys. Time can guide you toward new perspectives that may not be available without some distance. When I look back on my childhood now, I realize that my mom didn't do what she did to me because I was a "bad" kid or because I was unlovable. No, that's how she was disciplined, and the trauma her parents inflicted on her was also passed on to me. I realize that she didn't know that what she put me through could be traumatic, because what she'd been through had been so much worse. I realize that my mom may have been struggling with her own traumatic past that she hadn't yet healed from. I realize that when she lost her temper, I didn't deserve that treatment, even if I could have behaved better.

These were perspectives that have developed with time, and I'm grateful that distance has given me the opportunity to see things from a different point of view. But still, even with space and new perspectives, time didn't have the power to erase the trauma I endured.

"

Time can support your healing, but it isn't a solution.

"

Just like we can't ignore our traumatic experiences and expect to heal, we can't expect time to magically heal our wounds either. Trauma doesn't work itself out, and healing is not a passive activity that occurs by happenstance; it's an active process that only takes place if we're intentional about it.

Intention creates space for your healing. Without intention, you may not give yourself the time or make yourself emotionally available to mend your wounds. Without intention, it's easy to continue living life as is, waiting for a miracle to happen.

Take some time to think about some of your intentions for your healing journey. Putting your desires into words will bring more focus to your healing, and it can help you get clear about the direction you want to be going. In Chapter 5, we'll discuss activities that may help you get there, and your intentions also may help inform your decisions and prioritize what you want to work on.

Think about some of the challenges you've been dealing with. Maybe trauma has left you feeling fearful and paranoid, or maybe you're suffering from insomnia. Maybe you're feeling lonely because there isn't anyone in your life you can trust. Next, think about how you want to feel, and what you want to get out of healing. It could be living a more peaceful life with minimal symptoms of trauma or learning to love and trust yourself (or others) again. Maybe it's being able to revisit your past without intense fear or shame overtaking you.

It's okay to let yourself dream. When you're dealing with trauma, your world can shrink and life may feel like it's limited to your suffering, and it can be a challenge even to envision a way out. You may not get there how you imagine, but remember, healing *is* possible, and while encountering obstacles along your journey is inevitable, you're capable of achieving whatever your desires may be. Just try not to be hard on yourself if you're not progressing as quickly as you want to be. While time alone cannot heal, healing does take time (and work). But the time and effort you put into healing will be time well spent.

CHAPTER 3

your emotions are your allies

Trauma can make you feel like you're out of control. Unexpected triggers can transport you back to the most terrifying moment of your life, and suddenly, you may start panicking, screaming, or bursting into tears. You may feel paranoid, no matter who you are with and where you are—always on high alert, as danger could be around any corner. You may stay awake for days, not feeling safe enough to rest at night, because even in your sleep, your mind won't let you forget what happened. You may be questioning your reality because others don't recognize the same threats as you. You may feel like you've completely lost your mind.

If any of this sounds familiar, you aren't alone. There was a time when I *never* felt safe. I constantly looked over my shoulder when walking outside to make sure nobody was following me. When I returned to an empty home, I tiptoed throughout my house to make sure each room was clear, my thumb hovering over the panic button on my portable alarm. I triple-checked my doors and windows to make sure they were locked at night. I'd leap out of the shower with shampoo running into my eyes whenever I heard a noise, which my brain always registered as "danger." I'd jump at every knock at my door, holding my breath until I heard the visitor walk away, as I always believed the person on the other side must be someone coming to attack me.

Living with these symptoms can be painful, terrifying, and exhausting, and on top of that, you may feel ashamed. Because what I went through wasn't "that bad," I thought that I was weak for experiencing such symptoms. Because I couldn't just let it go and move on with my life, I thought that I was damaged. I thought that I was broken beyond repair, and that I'd just have to get used to living in fear.

I thought that the problem was *me*, when in reality, my brain and body were doing exactly what they were supposed to do: protect me.

Your brain isn't your enemy—it's your protector.

The fear and hypervigilance we experience after trauma can feel overwhelming, but healing isn't about getting rid of your fears altogether. Fear is a vital human emotion, and we need it to keep us safe. If we weren't afraid of cars speeding toward us as we cross a street, we wouldn't have the internal signal to tell us to run and get out of the way. Fear made my heart race as I stood at the ATM that morning in San Francisco, and it gave me a shot of adrenaline, preparing me to run for my life. During your traumatic experience(s), fear probably helped you survive too.

While our brains and bodies are doing their best to keep us safe, they can take it a step too far and be *overprotective*. Flashbacks and nightmares replay our traumatic experiences, reminding us of what has happened, to protect us from something similar happening again. To prepare ourselves for the worst-case scenario, we're on high alert, and may not allow ourselves to rest. Our minds generate frightening fantasies, warning us of potentially dangerous situations that could arise. Anxiety spikes and gives us a rush of adrenaline, so we're ready to fight or take flight. All senses are heightened to help us survive, even when we aren't in jeopardy.

At times, it may seem like these symptoms appear out of the blue, but they can often be traced back to a trigger. When we go through a traumatic experience, emotional and sensory information is stored in the brain and body (Van der Kolk, 2015). Memories of past traumas not only include where we were and what we saw, but also what we heard, smelled, tasted, and felt. When reminded of traumatic events from these internal or external cues (triggers), it activates our fight-flight-freeze survival response. Even if you're completely safe, your mind may read these cues as threats, and you might get hit by extreme fear.

Triggers show up differently for everyone. You might start panicking, panting, or hyperventilating; you might freeze like you're a statue and not be able to move or speak; or you might start yelling or screaming or breaking down in tears. When you're triggered, it may feel like you're reliving the traumatic experience all over again, and you might react just like you did during the event itself. On several occasions, I've sprinted down the street, running for my life after hearing block heels clapping on the concrete behind me. Getting triggered often feels like you're out of control as panic and explosive emotions surface within seconds. Or it may feel like you want to move or say something, but your body won't let you. It can feel like you're completely disconnected from reality, isolated in your own little world.

I always felt so ashamed for how I reacted after getting triggered. Even if nobody else saw me burst into tears, scream, run, or hide, I felt ridiculous once I realized the threat wasn't real. I'd think, *What the hell is wrong with me? Why did I react like that?* I judged myself, and I felt weak for not being able to stay calm or think rationally. I invalidated my feelings, but I should have shown myself more compassion. Getting triggered is an automatic and involuntary response, and when we're in survival mode, it's almost impossible to control our reactions. Getting triggered is genuinely terrifying. You aren't overreacting or being "dramatic": the fear is real.

Healing is so much more about understanding yourself than it is about changing yourself.

While it's important to recognize where there are opportunities for growth, when you criticize, judge, and shame yourself, it doesn't support your healing. Your symptoms are a natural response to trauma: your body evolved to help you survive. Experiencing trauma symptoms doesn't make you weak or damaged, and struggling with them isn't a personal failure. I know they may get in the way and make life so much more challenging, but we can't switch them off, and beating yourself up won't help you find relief any faster. If anything, it might add to the pain you're already feeling, making it harder to work through. When we criticize and shame ourselves, we sometimes get so stuck on what went wrong, or what we wish we could have done, that it keeps us from moving forward.

The next time you get triggered, or any of your trauma symptoms arise, remember to show yourself some compassion. If you feel frustrated, gently remind yourself that your brain and body are trying to protect you. Triggers can be anywhere, and since we can't control other people's actions and everything that happens in our environments, it's imperative to learn how to cope with them, especially if they're keeping you from carrying out your life.

Building self-awareness and developing a better understanding of your triggers and your symptoms is a great place to start. Take some time to observe what's happening, internally and externally. Take note of where you are and what you see, hear, and smell. Notice, without judgment, any thoughts that enter your mind, and any physical sensations. Write all your observations down, and then identify anything that reminds you of the traumatic event you experienced—if you are in a similar environment, hear a particular sound, catch a scent, or have the same emotions.

Connecting the dots and identifying the origins of your triggers is a huge step toward healing. It can help reduce the shame you may feel for getting triggered by something that seems trivial, and it will help you realize that your feelings make sense. It is possible to work through your triggers to desensitize them so they're easier to live with (exposure therapy helped me with that), but since trauma is deeply personal and all of our triggers are unique, we're not going to get into that here. But the more you understand your triggers, the more information you'll have to work through them.

You don't need to fix your emotions—you need to listen to them.

Even when a trigger isn't present, trauma often brings a mess of unwanted emotions: grief, confusion, shame, loneliness, frustration, and the list goes on. But a lot of the time, we don't let ourselves feel our true feelings.

Sometimes we judge ourselves because we believe we should or shouldn't feel a certain way. Sometimes we dismiss our feelings because they're inconvenient to entertain, and we need to carry on with our days. Some of us may numb our emotions so we don't have to feel the pain.

Sometimes we throw ourselves into work and activities to keep busy because sitting in discomfort is unbearable, and sometimes, we push our feelings away because we worry they would reveal we're weak or defective in some way.

I spent the first 28 years of my life avoiding my emotions. I didn't know how to identify my feelings or give voice to them. Most of the time, I wasn't even aware they existed because I was conditioned to lock them away.

I remember having my feelings dismissed a lot as a child. I believe I was born naturally sensitive, so I felt things more deeply, and when I didn't feel seen or heard, I'd get angry and would start yelling or burst into tears. I was often sent to my room for a time-out. I remember jumping up and down in excitement when I saw a chocolate cake my mom bought for someone's birthday (not mine), and my mom snapped at me and said, "Okay, that's enough!" Even happy emotions weren't always welcome. So, over time, I learned how to bury them.

The harder emotions that I didn't know how to navigate through would expand beneath the surface. Sometimes, it would get to the point where I blew up like a volcanic eruption and my anger and pain was unleashed in unhealthy and harmful ways: screaming at others, breaking glassware, kicking my dresser, destroying my room, cutting myself in my bathtub. Like many other survivors of childhood trauma, I didn't understand my emotions, and I didn't know how to handle them. That didn't change in my teens and twenties when I found ways to avoid my emotions through food, exercise, substances, work, and a busy social life.

I used to think that having feelings was a weakness and something that had to be fixed. In addition to having my feelings dismissed, friends would also tell me "you're sensitive," like it was a bad thing, because I didn't find an offensive joke funny, or because I failed to hold back a few tears while watching a movie. In recent years, I've learned that my sensitivity feeds my ability to be empathetic and passionate, and getting emotional isn't a weakness. We're *supposed* to have emotions; we're not robots. Having feelings doesn't mean something's wrong with you—it means you're human.

If you're starting to allow yourself to feel however you feel, you're healing.

Feeling Fuels Healing

Throughout your healing journey, you'll be confronted by a variety of emotions, some more intense and unpleasant than others. An essential part of healing is learning how to process all this, as pushing feelings away only makes them come back stronger. In my case, ignoring my fear and anxiety often led to panic, as my body begged me not to ignore my feelings for another minute. I know it can be terrifying to sit with your feelings, and I know it can be tempting to detach yourself to avoid pain. But when we constantly avoid our emotions, we disregard important information that can help us heal. Our feelings can be our most valuable teachers, and they can help us understand ourselves better, bringing our attention to areas where we need healing. And numbing through substances, work, exercise, partying, or nonstop planning may allow you to escape your feelings for a while, but that relief is temporary. Numbing isn't healing, so don't mistake feeling *less* for feeling *better*. Again, pain doesn't magically disappear, and we can't shut off our emotions forever (they'll make their way out in one way or another), so the only way to find true relief is to work through it.

Instead of pushing your emotions away, try to bring your attention to them with compassion and curiosity. When you become aware of your emotions, they start to lose their power. Since processing your emotions isn't something that's typically taught in school (or at home), most of us haven't learned how. I didn't have a clue where to start until I went to therapy, and if your emotions are overwhelming, you may find working with a professional helpful too. Here are some of the tips I've learned over the course of my healing journey.

Take a Break

When an intense emotion arises—whether anger, frustration, sadness, guilt, confusion, or embarrassment— take a moment to pause and give yourself some space. If a conversation is what provoked the emotion, step away from it if you can. If you feel panic starting to arise, focus on grounding yourself. Grounding techniques bring your attention back to what's going on "here and now" by activating your senses and engaging with your surroundings. There are dozens, if not thousands, of techniques you can try, and it might take some trial and error to figure out what is helpful to you. A few of my go-to techniques:

- Pet a furry friend, or touch something soft, and feel the texture on your fingertips.

- Study a photo or piece of art and say your observations out loud.

- Name five things you see, four things you can touch, three things you hear, two things you can smell, and one thing you can taste.

- Eat something or chew a piece of gum and notice the flavors.

- Hold a piece of ice and note how it feels.

Feel Your Feelings

Let yourself feel however you feel (safely!). Letting yourself express your emotions can help you self-soothe. If you need to scream, scream. If you need to cry, let the tears flow. Crying releases oxytocin, a hormone that can ease pain and promote calmness (Newhouse, "Is Crying Good for You?" *Harvard Health Publishing*, 2021), so even if you're left puffy-eyed, you'll most likely find some relief. If you feel angry and have an urge to hit or destroy something, to keep yourself and others safe, you could try going on a run, lifting weights, or doing another workout to release some of that energy.

Feeling your feelings also means letting yourself feel *good* too. So many of us may feel uncomfortable letting ourselves be happy or excited or proud or even content, because it doesn't feel safe. I was chased when I was enjoying myself, looking forward to the farmers' market and a beautiful fall day in Napa. Then suddenly, I was in danger. When I was sexually assaulted in college, I was carefree, having a fun night out at a club with my friends, then unexpectedly, the situation I was in was no longer safe. I had a similar experience the night my friend got assaulted at a restaurant in San Francisco. As a result of all these experiences, I started to associate joy and happiness with pain, and I sometimes find myself rejecting happiness to protect myself.

Dealing with ongoing trauma symptoms and living in constant fear can make unhappiness feel like the norm, which can make happiness feel unfamiliar and frightening when it comes around. Because of this it's important to practice feeling the good things as well. If you feel happy, even if just for a moment, let yourself smile. Let yourself laugh or do a happy dance. Healing is just as much about lingering in your happiness as it is about leaning into discomfort.

Observe Yourself

When you're overpowered with strong emotions but don't know why, it can be terrifying. Building self-awareness will help you understand your feelings better, so they feel less threatening when they arise. I've always found that writing through it helps me explore my emotions, and it also helps me feel lighter as I release them onto the page. A few questions to ask yourself:

- *What am I feeling?* This question can be a tough one, especially if you've spent most of your life suppressing or avoiding your emotions. You can use a feelings list or an emotion wheel (Google it!), and scan through it to see what fits. Sometimes, we can feel multiple things at the same time, and that's completely natural. If you're new to this, identifying your feelings takes practice, but over time, it'll come more easily.

- *Where in my body am I feeling it?* Sometimes our emotions can activate sensations in our body. For example, when we're excited, many of us get the "butterflies in the stomach" feeling. If you're angry or embarrassed, you might feel your face heat up, and when anxious, you may feel tightness in your chest or knots in your stomach. If you're afraid or stressed, you might have stomach pain or digestive issues. When I ignore my emotions (sometimes unintentionally), they tend to get my attention through physical sensations, so building body awareness can help identify which emotions you're feeling and might be suppressing.

- *What is contributing to how I feel?* Think back to the moment when the feeling emerged. Was there something that activated it? If nothing is coming to mind, think of anything else that happened that day. Think of any memories that surfaced, or a thought or image that appeared in your mind that may have induced the feeling. Maybe you had a stressful day at work, or you went to a place that made you feel unsafe. Maybe something reminded you of your trauma. The more awareness you have around what triggers your emotions, the better understanding you'll have around your feelings, which can help you identify which needs aren't being met, or where you might need to set boundaries. (We'll discuss this more in Chapter 5 and Chapter 10.)

Validate Your Feelings

Accept how you feel in the moment. I've found that fighting with my feelings, trying to "fix" them, or telling myself *I shouldn't feel this way* only creates more tension and pain, making it more challenging for me to work through them. If you feel an urge to judge yourself for having feelings, that's natural. So many of us learned at a young age that there are good and bad emotions, and the bad ones should be locked away. People think that anger is a "negative" emotion, as it's associated with aggression and violence. But just like fear, anger is a natural emotion that prepares us to defend ourselves, and it can tell us when something feels wrong or unfair. For many others and me, anger has fueled our activism. Anger can be healing, too, as it notifies us when our boundaries have been violated and often gives us the fuel to stand up for ourselves.

Feelings aren't good or bad—they're just feelings—and you're allowed to feel however you feel. Feeling a certain way doesn't mean you're weak or dramatic or a bad person; it means you're having a natural, human response to something. It only becomes an issue if you respond to your feelings with actions that hurt yourself or others. Letting go of the belief that what you're feeling is wrong will make your feelings easier to sit with and validate.

Comfort Yourself

Feeling and exploring your emotions, especially the difficult ones, may be confusing, frightening, and draining, so it's important to soothe and comfort yourself so you can move forward. Finding comfort is a challenge when you're being judgmental or dismissive, or telling yourself how you should and shouldn't feel, so remember to show yourself compassion. Tell yourself things like, *This is hard. I know you're in pain. It makes sense why you feel this way. We're going to get through this.* Take a few deep breaths. Give yourself a big bear hug. Make yourself a cup of tea. Treat yourself like you would someone you care for who's having a hard day.

Take Action

Our feelings aren't fixed; eventually, they will pass, although, depending on what you're dealing with, they may hang around for a while. Sometimes, we need to do something to make ourselves feel better so we can move forward. After all, many of us have responsibilities to fulfill that we need to be able to return to. For instance, if you got into an argument with someone earlier, you may need to make amends, or express something to them, to feel better. I know that if Adam and I get in a fight, it's impossible for me to fall asleep without reconciling with him. Or maybe you need to call someone you can vent to, or who can help you brainstorm solutions to a problem you're facing. Talking things through with someone who is empathetic grounds me, and almost always helps me feel better. If you're feeling restless, getting some fresh air and going on a walk or run, or going to the park to shoot hoops or kick a ball around may help you feel more at ease. If you're feeling down, you could try dancing and singing along to a favorite song, or maybe a soothing activity like drawing or cooking would provide much-needed comfort. Again, it can take some experimentation to figure out what's most helpful so you aren't stuck in the feeling for too long.

It's Okay to Take a Break

There will be times when you may not be able to go through this whole process and "feel your feelings," and that's okay. There are times when I need to contain my emotions to get through the day due to work and meetings, and I don't have a choice but to push them away. Sometimes I feel like I really need to cry when I'm in public, but I need to wait until I'm in a safe space to let it out. Sometimes I feel overwhelmed due to what's happening in my life and the world, and I just need to tune my feelings out. Sometimes our emotions are too much to handle, and we may not have the time, space, or support to process them safely. Give yourself permission to distance yourself from your feelings from time to time, but try not to leave them on the back burner for too long. Otherwise, they may start spilling over and make a mess that affects all areas of your life.

Changing the way we relate to our pain changes the way we live with it.

While trauma symptoms are natural, human responses, when they hit you, it certainly doesn't feel "normal." I know it can sometimes feel like there's something seriously wrong with you when you get extremely upset or frightened over something that seems trivial. Others who don't understand triggers and the toll trauma can take on a person might make you feel that way too. But there is nothing wrong with *you*—what's wrong is what happened *to* you, and your brain and body are trying to protect you from it happening again.

While the pain won't disappear, once you stop battling yourself and your feelings, the pain won't feel as severe. Understanding your triggers and how they affect you can help you release your self-judgment. Understanding that you're allowed to feel however you feel can make difficult emotions easier to sit with. Showing yourself compassion throughout all of it will allow you to process what you're feeling and experiencing, instead of avoiding it due to judgment and shame.

You are not broken or damaged, and you don't need fixing. You are hurt, in pain, and you need healing. It is possible to live symptom-free after trauma, but it may take some time. Shifting the way you perceive your symptoms, triggers, and feelings changes the way you live them, and it can help you feel better now, even if just by an inch.

CHAPTER 4

you weren't meant to heal alone

I've always been independent. My parents like to remind me that the first sentence I strung together was "leave me alone" while I was watching *The Jungle Book*. Even at 18 months old, I knew when I needed my space. They tell me that when I was two years old, instead of letting them carry a backpack that was too heavy for me, I stubbornly lugged it along until I tipped over and fell on my back. For as long as I can remember, I wore my independence with pride: I thought it made me a better, stronger, more accomplished person.

I believed that asking for help and not knowing things made me weak and incompetent, so I never did it. When I was in school, I refused to raise my hand in class or go to my teacher when I was having a hard time following along. I thought that if I voiced that I didn't understand something, I'd get made fun of by my classmates for being dumb, or get accused of not paying attention by my teacher. I didn't ask my parents for help either. I preferred to struggle on my own to avoid criticism.

My approach was no different when it came to my mental health struggles. Up until I was about 25 years old, I didn't even know mental health was a thing. I had struggled with anxiety and depression throughout my entire life but never realized it, and I thought that my internal struggles reflected a personal failure. I thought that the issue was *me*, and that for people like me, life would always be hard, and it wasn't meant to be enjoyable. I thought that for people like me, happiness or love or success was unattainable.

I had been ashamed of myself for my entire life, but by the time I was 20 years old, my shame reached an all-time high. At 18, when I was a freshman in college, I partied most nights of the week. I was slut-shamed by a friend for hooking up with people I met when we were out at bars. During the spring semester, the university kicked me out of my dorm for smoking weed behind the building, and for my entire sophomore year, I lived alone off-campus. I wasn't allowed to step foot in housing on-campus, which was where all but one of my friends lived and hung out. While I managed to sneak into their dorms at times, I felt like all of my friends had moved on without me. They made new friendships and grew closer to one another, as I was left out of plans and often forgotten about.

That summer, I flew across the country and went back home to California. A few weeks before I was supposed to fly back for the fall semester, the guy from school I was dating told me he was going to visit his grandmother with his family for his birthday. He told me, "My grandma hates it when I'm on my phone, so I won't be able to text you for the next few days." *That's suspicious,* I thought. We had texted every single day for over six months and family had never gotten in the way. I called his home line on his birthday, when he said his whole family would be out of town, and after a few rings, I heard his mom's voice. I caught him in a lie, and when I confronted him about it, he confessed that he went on a road trip to go hook up with his ex-girlfriend. I was shocked, and my heart was in pain—it felt like it literally broke—and hives suddenly appeared on my chest. I was devastated.

After doing some light research on Facebook, I saw that his ex was pretty and thinner than me. I thought he'd betrayed me because I wasn't attractive enough, smart enough, or fun enough, and I felt like a failure because I couldn't fulfill his needs. I thought it was my fault, like something I did or didn't do drove him away. Shame kept me from telling any of my friends at school about it, and I suffered through the pain alone.

Life wasn't getting any better for me, and I felt hopeless. Each day was a struggle, and I had to force myself to get out of bed. Sometimes I couldn't bring myself to sit through class, so I ended up cutting many of them. For one accounting course where I knew the professor didn't take attendance, I only showed up three times the entire semester. Even though I walked around with a fake smile, pretending to be okay, I was miserable. Suicidal thoughts started seeping into my mind, and because I knew people viewed suicide as a weak, cowardly, sinful move, I tried my best to ignore them.

When I went back home for winter break, I checked my grades and saw that I hadn't passed the final for one of my classes, and it brought my grade down to a C. I felt stupid and worthless, like I couldn't do anything right, and I didn't know how I'd face my parents. Soon, the thoughts I'd tried to push away started flooding in. I felt like I was drowning, and I just wanted someone to be there for me, to throw me a life vest, but I didn't think that I had anyone to turn to. I wanted friends and family to comfort me, but deep down, I believed that I was unlovable. I believed I was a burden and that everyone would be better off without me. They didn't know I needed support, and I didn't know how to ask for it. I was scared to ask for it. What if I wasn't taken seriously? What if my pain was dismissed? What if I was judged or criticized? What if they confirmed that I am in fact not worthy of love or anything good in life? I didn't think it was worth the risk, and believed they wouldn't care anyway, so I decided to give up.

When I woke up in the hospital on Christmas Eve, nobody knew that I had attempted suicide. While I was devastated that I hadn't been successful, a part of me was relieved that nobody knew how I had ended up there. I didn't want them to judge me and call me "crazy" or "weak-minded," and I didn't want to be sent to a psychiatric hospital. But at the same time, I was incredibly lonely, and I wish someone knew how much I was suffering. I wanted someone to offer to help me, because I didn't know how to ask for it myself.

Needing help doesn't make you weak or needy— it makes you human.

99

I wish I knew that it was okay to be struggling. I wish I knew that I'm not expected to be perfect, and my past experiences don't define me. I wish I knew that I wasn't weak or a bad person for feeling suicidal, and for many of us, mental health struggles are part of the human experience. I wish I knew that I wasn't alone, and that help was available. Had I known those things, it might have been easier for me to reach out to someone.

Back then, I didn't know that therapy was an option for me—partly because I didn't know that I was struggling with my mental health, and partly because I hadn't heard anyone around me talking about therapy, online or in real life. Now I can't go on social media without seeing a post about therapy or trauma; things are different now, and I'm thankful for that.

I don't recall having any negative views about therapy, but I just didn't think that it was *for me*. I thought that it was for people who had been through things that were worse, like a devastating loss, *extreme* trauma, or a chronic illness. I also thought that therapy was a thing for rich white ladies who wanted someone they could complain to. My mother, who survived some of the most intense traumatic experiences I'd ever heard of, never went to therapy. She was building a beautiful new life in America and wasn't interested in looking back to revisit her terrifying past. Mental health wasn't ever a concern when she was living through the devastation following the Vietnam War—survival was the only priority—and it remained the priority as she adjusted to life in a new country. She didn't know that if you've had hard life experiences, going to therapy could help you process them and relieve your pain. Neither did I.

I didn't think about going to therapy until I was 28, when my trauma symptoms appeared in full force. And actually, if Adam hadn't asked, "Do you want to talk to someone?" after seeing me suffer day after day, I'm not sure how long it would have taken me to consider it.

Many of us who grew up in households where mental health was never discussed don't have a full picture of what therapy entails. When I started therapy, I thought that it might be a waste of time. Many of my anxiety symptoms were physiological—racing heart, shortness of breath, nausea, digestive issues—and I didn't see how talking about it would make the discomfort disappear. And after going to a doctor who ran all the tests and told me that I was completely healthy *physically*, I felt like I was running out of options, and knew it was time to give therapy a try.

I quickly learned that therapy involved so much more than venting to someone. It took a few sessions for me to feel comfortable with my therapist, but once I started to warm up to her, I appreciated having someone in my life that I met with on a weekly basis who was compassionate and nonjudgmental. She gave me her undivided attention, making me feel heard and seen—something I hadn't always experienced within my existing relationships. Even with a supportive partner, it was incredibly helpful to have someone else on my team with whom I could discuss the challenges in my life.

Within the first few months, my therapist helped me develop skills that have assisted me along my healing journey and with every other aspect of my life. I learned how to identify my feelings and how to process them. She taught me several breathing exercises that I could try out to quell my anxiety. She taught me coping exercises and ways I could ground myself when panic arises and ways

I can self-regulate when I'm feeling overwhelmed. She helped me confront my triggers so they no longer resulted in panic attacks every time. She helped me feel safe in my home and body again.

I don't have too many regrets on my healing journey, but one of them is not seeing a therapist sooner. I waited until the point when my trauma symptoms were so intense that I had no choice but to get professional help; had I gotten help sooner, I would've saved myself months of suffering from panic attacks and sleepless nights. I wish I had reached out for help after my suicide attempt. Knowing what I know about therapy now, it would have changed my life for the better, and I would have started healing from that experience years earlier.

I went through the most painful time of my life alone, but you don't have to.

Finding People to Help You Heal

Dealing with trauma can be so overwhelming that it's impossible to navigate through healing alone. At the beginning of your healing journey, you may be dealing with a range of disruptive symptoms, and you may not know where to start. While your loved ones are an invaluable part of your healing, unless they've been trained to do so, they don't have the capabilities to help you work through your trauma and treat your symptoms. While they can certainly provide comfort and help you feel less alone, even if they've been through a similar situation, you still may be facing different challenges. Trauma can manifest in many ways, and working with a mental health professional to help you tackle your unique challenges can be a game-changer.

If you have no clue where to start when it comes to seeking treatment, you aren't alone. I didn't know the difference between a psychologist or psychiatrist, or if there was a specific type of therapy I should try. Both psychologists and psychiatrists are involved in mental health treatment, but the main difference is that psychiatrists can prescribe medication, which psychologists and licensed therapists cannot do. If you want to explore medication options, set up a consultation with a psychiatrist to see what might be helpful for the symptoms you're experiencing. Otherwise, a psychologist or a licensed therapist is likely a good place to start; they can always refer you to a psychiatrist if needed. Even if medication is part of your treatment plan, therapy will most likely be part of it as well. As my psychiatrist told me, "There's no magic pill that cures trauma."

FINDING A THERAPIST

Try to find a therapist who is trauma-informed or specializes in PTSD and other trauma-related conditions. Unfortunately, not every therapist out there is qualified to help trauma survivors. I've heard hundreds of stories about therapists who have blamed trauma survivors for their traumatic experiences, dismissed their pain, made them feel unsafe, and further retraumatized them by pushing too hard. Not every therapist is a good therapist, and some may end up causing more harm. You don't have to settle for a therapist just because they're a therapist; there are plenty of options out there.

It's also important to note that not every therapist will be the right fit for you. When the process requires you to be vulnerable with someone, your preferences matter.

Based on my past experiences, it was hard for me to feel safe around men, so they were out of the question for me. I also wanted my therapist to be a person of color, so they'd better understand my experience as a mixed person. While these kinds of specifications will shrink your pool of potential providers, it's important to find someone you believe you'll feel comfortable opening up to.

Thanks to the "Find a Therapist" tools on sites like Psychology Today and GoodTherapy, finding a therapist that matches your preferences doesn't have to be too difficult. These tools not only allow you to filter by your insurance carrier and treatment focus, but also by the therapist's gender, language, faith, sexuality, and ethnicities served. While these tools don't capture every therapist in your area, they make it easy to sift through potential providers, and odds are, you'll find some promising leads.

All therapists have different treatment styles and belief systems, so I always encourage people to not give up on therapy just yet if they don't have a good experience on the first few tries. And it may take several sessions to even feel safe enough to open up to your therapist. For some of us, it can be a process learning how to trust others when we've been deeply harmed by other people before. However, for some people, therapy might not be helpful at all. Some survivors have shared with me that they've seen 10, 14, even 20 therapists, and tried every type of therapy they could, and none of them seemed to help. Some have shared that they've gotten more out of support groups and other types of community support. As neuroscientist and psychiatrist Dr. Bruce D. Perry explains in the book he wrote with Oprah Winfrey, *What Happened to You?*, "Most healing happens in *community*" (Perry and Winfrey, 2021). A healthy community provides ongoing, nurturing interactions that can be therapeutic.

SUPPORT GROUPS

When you feel isolated and think nobody in your life will understand what you're going through, connecting with other people who are facing similar challenges can be incredibly validating. When I was diagnosed with PTSD, I didn't know anyone else in my life who was living with the condition, so I joined an online "Women with PTSD" support group. Even though every one of us there had different traumatic experiences and came from different backgrounds, our symptoms and challenges often over-lapped. Just knowing that I wasn't alone helped release some of my shame and brought a level of comfort that my therapist or anyone else in my life couldn't provide. Sometimes you just need to talk to others who have been through it and can empathize with you.

Support groups take place in person or online, and many are led by licensed therapists who create a safe and supportive space. Some therapists provide psychoedu-cation in their support groups, so you can gain a better understanding of your symptoms and learn some coping skills. Each group is structured differently, and many of them cater to specific communities, like survivors of sex-ual assault, BIPOC trauma survivors, or survivors of birth trauma. Some groups may focus on a specific healing tech-nique, like trauma-conscious yoga, developing mindful-ness skills, or using creative practices like writing and art to heal. With the widely available options, you can likely find a group that speaks to you.

While you won't get one-on-one treatment with a therapist in a group setting, you'll have the opportunity to connect with other survivors and support one another, which is healing in its own way. Another support group plus: they're typically low-cost and sometimes free.

MENTAL HEALTH SUPPORT FOR EVERY BUDGET

I believe that everyone should have access to the health care they deserve, but I know this is not the reality for many. I've been so fortunate to have a decent health-care plan throughout my healing journey, but when professional support depends on one's employment, insurance coverage, and economic status, it's not readily available to everyone. Everyone should be able to access the support they need—it should be a right, not a resource that only those of us with privilege can afford.

Thousands of people in my Instagram community have expressed that the cost of therapy is the main reason why they haven't gotten professional help yet, and I get it. Therapy can be very expensive, even if you have insurance coverage. The good news is, there are providers and organizations that are closing the treatment gap, so even if you are in a financially stressful situation, you can still have a professional by your side. This is not a complete list, but here are a few things you can look into:

- *Sliding Scale Therapy.* Some therapists offer a flexible fee structure where the cost of your therapy sessions depends on your income. For example, if a therapist's full fee is $150 for each session, depending on your income, you may pay $100 or $60, and if you're in a particularly tough financial situation, you may pay nothing. It's important to note that getting a discounted rate doesn't mean you'll be getting a lower level of service. Therapists want to help people—it's what they do—and they recognize that people who are better off are at an advantage when it comes to treatment, which is why they offer a pay-what-you-can solution. The clients that pay full price help balance things out, so therapists can offer lower rates to others. The "Find a Therapist" tools I mentioned earlier allow you to filter by therapists who offer sliding scales.

- *Nonprofits.* There are several organizations with a mission to make mental health care more accessible to those who need it. Open Path Psychotherapy Collective partners with clinicians to provide low-cost therapy services to individuals and families with rates starting at $30 per session. NeedyMeds keeps a database of free, low-cost, and sliding scale clinics, where you can search for support in your city and state. Community-focused organizations, like The Loveland Foundation and National Queer and Trans Therapists of Color Network, have therapy funds, offering financial assistance for community members who need mental health care.

- *Schools and Universities.* If you're in school, check to see what resources you have at your health center. Your school may offer free individual or group therapy sessions on-campus, or they may be able to refer you to a therapist off-campus who offers a sliding scale fee. Even if you aren't a student, if you live near a university hospital, they're often looking for new patients for training programs for their grad students, interns, and residents, where you can get low- or no-cost mental health care.

LET SOMEONE HELP YOU

Trying to find mental health support when you're struggling might feel like an impossible task. For me, finding a therapist was so stressful that it brought on a panic attack. One afternoon, I called and e-mailed 15 providers and had no luck finding one that accepted my insurance and was taking on new clients. I grew frustrated with the entire process. I was dizzy flipping between tabs as I cross-referenced psychologists listed on my insurance carrier's website with the psychologists' websites, frantically trying to find someone who seemed like a good fit. My heart started pounding as I thought, *What if I can't find anyone? I'm never going to get help. I'm going to have to live like this for the rest of my life!* Then I burst into tears, and panic swooped in and stole the last sliver of energy I had left that day.

When Adam got home from work, he found me curled up under a chunky knit blanket on the couch, drinking herbal tea and watching *The Office*. I cried as I told him, "I can't find anyone to help me. I don't know what to do. I just want to feel normal again."

He sat next to me and put his arm around my shoulder and said, "Let me help you."

Those were the best words I'd heard all week.

When you're anxious and in panic mode, the smallest tasks can become a huge challenge. When your thoughts are spiraling and you're on the verge of tears, it's impossible to concentrate. The simplest answer could be sitting right in front of you, but it's easy to overlook when you're overwhelmed with trauma symptoms. Adam made it seem so easy. Within ten minutes, he found five providers in our network who matched my preferences—something that would've taken me an hour. And the thing is, he didn't have a different strategy or anything; he was doing the exact same thing I'd been doing. He was just more efficient because he wasn't dealing with constant anxiety. He also didn't have the discouragement of prior rejections weighing on him; he was in a better state of mind. Together, we reached out to all the providers Adam had found. I was relieved the next day when one of the psychologists e-mailed me back, telling me she had availability to take me on as a patient.

If I'd asked for Adam's help in finding a therapist sooner (like when he suggested that I try therapy), it probably would've prevented that panic attack from happening. If there is someone in your life you can trust—a significant other, sibling, mentor, parent, co-worker, or another doctor you see—ask them to help you out with this. Spend some time thinking about the best person to go to, and what you'd want to say to them in advance. You don't have to tell them about your trauma (we'll discuss that more in Chapter 9), and while it's helpful to provide some context, it's best to keep it short and specific, so the ask is clear. You could say something along the lines of, "My anxiety has been awful lately, and I want to try therapy, but I'm having no luck finding someone. The stress is overwhelming. I could really use your help finding a provider." I know it can be scary to reach out to others for help, especially when you don't want to feel needy, or feel like you'll be judged, but if you think someone's assistance can relieve some of your stress, it's worth it to ask.

The stigma formerly associated with therapy has melted away as people have increasingly embraced and prioritized mental health. People now go to therapy for preventive care or to explore areas of personal growth, even when something isn't explicitly "wrong." While most people may not talk about therapy in everyday conversations, there is almost certainly *someone* in your life who has been to therapy, has been involved in a support group, or has seen a psychiatrist and understands how challenging it can be to find the right support. If you're lost and overwhelmed, ask someone you trust for help, and they'll likely help you find your way.

Some people don't realize how hard it is to ask for help, and how much courage it takes for one to open up about their struggles. If someone shuts you down, invalidates your feelings, or dismisses your cries for help, claiming you "just want attention," know that you deserve so much better. Their reaction is not a reflection of you. Allowing yourself to be vulnerable with someone who has no compassion for what you're going through isn't a failure on your end; it's a limitation on the other person's end. If someone judges you for struggling, or for not being able to handle something on your own, ask yourself, *Is it worth it to continue investing in this relationship?*

Asking for help doesn't mean you're weak or incompetent; having enough self-awareness to recognize your limits is a sign of strength. Recognizing your full humanity and letting others get a glimpse of it is an act of bravery. When the world constantly tells us who we should be and what's acceptable, it takes courage to show up as we are—as our authentic, imperfect selves. I know it may be tempting to keep your struggles to yourself in an effort to protect yourself, but healing isn't about hiding, containing, or controlling: it's about liberating yourself.

If you're learning to ask for and accept help, you're healing.

"

I'm still working on being more vulnerable; for me, it's an ongoing practice. It's still hard for me to ask for help when I'm lost and overwhelmed, or when I'm longing for comfort and validation. Sometimes I open up about a problem I'm having, but I have a hard time saying that I could use help. But I'm finding that it becomes easier with practice. Once you ask for support a couple of times, it doesn't feel like as big of a deal when you ask again in the future.

I used to think that it would be the absolute worst thing if anyone knew I was struggling, but one thing I've learned these past few years is that letting our loved ones in on what we're going through can provide us with the support we're craving. When I've expressed that I'm having a hard time, other people have helped me feel seen and heard. Letting tears run down my cheeks has prompted much-needed hugs. Sometimes letting people see our struggles makes us feel more connected and less alone. I used to think that relationships were all about being happy together and enjoying each other's company, but I've learned that the best relationships are those where you can also lean on others to help you through the rough patches.

We weren't built to know everything, or to figure everything out on our own. We weren't built to push through our pain in isolation and heal alone. Whenever you're feeling overwhelmed or helpless and things get too heavy, reach out for help and let someone lighten your load.

CHAPTER 5

there are no shortcuts

Three weeks into therapy, I questioned whether it was going to work for me. My anxiety was still out of control, I was still waking up in the middle of the night in a panic, and I didn't have a diagnosis yet. We weren't getting anywhere.

During our first session, I explained the symptoms I was experiencing to my therapist, who then asked, "Has anything happened that was terrifying? Or have you lost anyone?"

I scanned my memories for 20 seconds or so, and only one thing stood out. "My grandpa passed away a couple years ago, but we weren't that close. He lived across the country." Sometimes our minds make it more challenging to retrieve our traumatic memories so it's easier to carry out our lives.

During that first session, I shared more about my relationships, work, and bits of what I could remember from my childhood. I gave her the Instagram version of my life story (my accomplishments and the happier occasions) and Photoshopped the rest out. I wasn't comfortable with the whole client-therapist relationship yet, and I feared that I'd face judgment or rejection if I shared my flaws. I wanted to be a "good" therapy client, which I thought meant being the most impressive version of myself.

Since getting my anxiety and panic under control was a high priority for me, my therapist walked me through some breathing exercises and ways I could ground myself during our first few sessions. She explained that practicing deep breathing is important, because when you're anxious, your breath is short, but taking in more oxygen can help soften your pounding heart, shakiness, and other anxiety symptoms. It made sense, but none of her techniques seemed to work. Some even felt like they made my anxiety worse, and I wondered if I might be wasting my time. I thought about quitting, but decided to keep trying because I *needed* to feel better, and I didn't have a plan B.

I let her know that the breathing exercises weren't working. "I tried them all. Nothing is helping," I told her.

She then asked, "When you tried them, how did they feel?"

I explained that I tried them when my anxiety spiked, and it felt like I was on the verge of panic. "They weren't making the sensation in my chest disappear, and when I noticed how the exercises weren't working, I'd get frustrated, and then my heart would pound faster."

She slowly nodded and gently said, "I see."

She then explained that if I don't practice the exercises when I'm calmer and only test them out as a lifeline, they might backfire and make my anxiety worse. "Breathing and mindfulness and any other coping skills you learn here will take practice."

Oh, I thought. That's when I started to realize that healing lies in my hands.

Healing isn't about following someone else's blueprint—it's about creating your own.

I went into therapy with the unrealistic expectation that my therapist would just figure out what was wrong with me, and then she'd work some therapist magic, and voilà—I'd be fixed. Even when we'd started discussing my trauma a few weeks later, I thought that showing up to therapy and working through it for 45 minutes each week would be enough to help me heal. I thought that answering her questions and participating during the sessions would be enough for my therapist to make me feel better right away.

Even though my therapist showed me coping skills in session, it was my responsibility to practice them. And once I did start practicing them, I found a breathing exercise (box breathing) and a mindfulness exercise (body scan) that helped me feel calmer. Once I consistently started putting more effort into therapy, my symptoms weren't as intense, and they showed up less frequently, and I began finding relief.

After more than three years of trauma therapy, I can tell you that 98 percent of my healing has happened outside of therapy. That isn't because therapy isn't valuable, or that my therapists weren't good at their jobs—I've been very fortunate to work with a few fantastic therapists. So much of the work that goes into therapy happens *outside* of therapy, and just showing up isn't enough. It was up to me to practice the coping skills at home in order to identify ones that I could depend on. In my own time, I worked to build self-awareness to better understand myself so I could then relay information to my therapist for my treatment. I practiced rewriting the endings of my terrifying dreams each night until my nightmares became rare. Even though she introduced me to so many techniques that helped me cope with PTSD, they wouldn't have been nearly as effective had I not put the work in myself. Had I not created a soothing environment outside of therapy, doing the deep trauma work inside of therapy would have been too overwhelming.

It's also unrealistic to think that your therapist, or any other person out there, can fulfill every healing need that you have; there isn't one person (or activity) that can make your pain disappear. When you only see someone for one hour each week, to keep things moving you need to find ways to support your healing for the other 167 hours in the week. A lot of people have this idea that therapy is the *only* path to healing, and that therapists are the only people who can help you heal. That simply isn't true. Healing isn't just about decreasing your symptoms; it's about feeling at home within yourself. Part of healing is working toward feeling more empowered, forming supportive relationships, finding what brings you joy, and becoming someone who feels true to you. This piece requires you to turn inward and take action, and while therapists can certainly support you, this is *your* life, and you're in the best position to lead the way.

One of the most healing activities for me has been using my voice to share my story and advocate for others like me—it's made me feel empowered and has reduced my shame in ways I never thought would be possible. Connecting with other trauma survivors and cultivating nurturing relationships has also been incredibly healing as it's helped me feel seen and supported. Daily self-care—rest, quiet time, fresh air, breaking a sweat, cuddles, prioritizing sleep—has helped me feel more at ease and has provided much-needed relief from the chaos that trauma brings. Tapping into my creativity has brought me joy and has helped me feel alive again after being weighed down by my past. While therapy played a critical role in my healing journey, it didn't completely transform me into the person I am today. Creating my own healing environment outside of therapy that has helped me feel empowered, safe, supported, and connected has been just as, if not more, beneficial.

When I first started healing, I thought that my therapist was in the driver's seat, and I was just along for the ride. I wanted her to give me the answers and tell me what to do because that felt easier than making decisions myself. But healing isn't about following someone's else's blueprint; it's about creating your own to fit *your* needs. After all, you are the most qualified to make decisions on what's best for you; there isn't another person on earth who knows your trauma, challenges, and desires better than you.

On your healing journey, you're the one behind the wheel; your therapist, partner, and anyone else are people you can lean on for support along the way. And while you'll run into some obstacles and may not have a clue what you're doing at times, the journey is much more rewarding when you're the one paving the way.

There's No Single Fix

With trauma, so many of us have searched for the simple solution to heal our wounds, whether it's the "best" type of therapy, a medication, or the most beneficial practices. I wish there was one single type of therapy that could cure everyone's trauma, and I wish healing was as simple as taking a pill or doing yoga; it would make things so much less complicated and confusing. But trauma is complex, and there are many layers involved, so a one-size-fits-all approach would never work for all of us. And as unique individuals with different backgrounds, experiences, and needs, we must make our healing journeys uniquely our own.

Finding what helps you heal takes some trial and error. For example, there are so many types of trauma therapy one could try, including Eye Movement Desensitization and Reprocessing (EMDR), Cognitive Behavioral Therapy (CBT), Dialectical Behavioral Therapy (DBT), Exposure Therapy, Somatic Therapy, and many more. Some survivors have found huge success with CBT, while for others, it wasn't helpful at all. Some people have told me, "EMDR saved my life," while others have shared that the process was so triggering that they quit after trying to stick it out for a few months. Just because someone found success with one type of trauma treatment doesn't guarantee that it'll work just as well for you, and in contrast, someone might find a particular type of therapy completely useless while it ends up being beneficial for you. You can read up about your options in advance, but most likely, you won't know if something helps your healing unless you try it yourself.

While there isn't a substitute for clinical work with a professional, it may not be as helpful for some people at certain points on their healing journeys (or at all), and that's okay. It may cause more pain to keep trying to force something that isn't working—that may just make you feel frustrated and discouraged, tempting you to give up on healing altogether.

Let go of what you believe your healing journey should look like and what you think you should or shouldn't be doing to heal. Sometimes, because we believe healing needs to work a certain way, we try to force things on ourselves that don't serve us. Again, there are so many paths you could take, and if something doesn't seem to be helping you, there are always other options. The key to healing is finding a combination of things that best serve you and your current needs.

Identifying Your Needs

For most of my life, I felt like I wasn't allowed to have needs. As a kid, I felt like I had to do whatever my parents wanted me to do because I believed my worthiness was based on my ability to live up to my parents' expectations. And when I got into the "real world" and started working, I was an unimportant entry-level employee at the bottom of the corporate ladder who had to do whatever I was told—my needs (or ideas or voice) didn't matter. I didn't really start paying attention to my needs until I began healing and realized that my needs matter too.

When our needs aren't met, it can cause additional stress and pain. For example, when we're deprived of food, a basic need, hunger often leads to a grumbling stomach, dizziness, low energy, and irritability. But once we have a meal, we feel more content, and those symptoms start fading away. The same can happen with our emotional needs. When they're not met, we're often left feeling anxious, lonely, trapped, or distressed, adding to the pain we're already feeling from the trauma we've endured. If you've never paid attention to your needs before, identifying them will take some practice, but as you begin listening to and fulfilling your needs regularly, the pain may feel less intense.

I know this may start to feel like a running theme since self-awareness is important for so many aspects of healing, but it's also the key to identifying your needs. Our feelings act as a guide when determining what our needs are, and we can't tune into our emotions without self-awareness. So often, when we check in with ourselves, we only notice our surface-level emotions (sad, angry, tired, happy, stressed, afraid), and while this is a great place to start, it's beneficial to explore one level deeper to pinpoint our true feelings.

For example, I often felt stressed at work. But it wasn't just stress; I felt overworked, overwhelmed, and underappreciated. When I was sad after getting in an argument with Adam, I really felt disconnected, lonely, and misunderstood. After a fun day with friends, I'd feel happy, but I also felt heard, connected, and grateful. When I felt tired but wasn't sleepy, I often felt bored and numb.

When a strong emotion arises, take a moment to observe yourself, as we discussed in Chapter 3. If you're feeling stuck trying to name your true feelings, you might find it helpful to scribble down every potential emotion you could be feeling in a notebook, even if what you write doesn't feel completely on point. Think of it like a brainstorming session. Then you will be able to narrow down your list until you're left with what feels most accurate. Again, identifying these underlying feelings takes practice, so be patient with yourself throughout this process, but the more specific you get with your feelings, the easier it is to identify your needs.

Once you've determined your true feelings, use that information to ask yourself, *What do I need right now? Is this something I can provide myself, or do I need it from someone else?*

Say you're feeling disconnected and lonely. That might mean that you need connection, whether it be spiritual, or with a person or community. If you're feeling overworked and overwhelmed, maybe you need to set boundaries to give yourself time to recharge, or maybe you need someone to assist you with something. If you're feeling distressed, empty, and alone, you may need some emotional support, whether through therapy, a support group, or a friend. If you're feeling bored and numb, you may be craving some creativity. If you're feeling anxious and disorganized, a daily practice like journaling, mindfulness, or yoga may help you feel more grounded. If you're feeling irritable and restless, a soothing activity like a walk outside, soaking in a warm bath, or letting tears stream from your eyes may help you feel calmer. These are all just suggestions, because, again, you're the most qualified to determine what feels best for you.

Show Up for Yourself

Once you determine your needs, you can now figure out how to meet those needs. It may take some experimentation to see what actions fulfill your needs and help you feel better. As you start trying things out, take note of how you feel afterward. Remember, as in my case with the breathing exercises, it might take some practice before something sticks. But if you try an approach a few times and it always leaves you feeling worse, don't force it; there are several other options out there, and not everything is going to serve you at every given time.

If something doesn't work out, it isn't necessarily a waste of time. You can use the information you gain about yourself (what you didn't like about it, what you did) to determine what you want to try next. If you found something that helped you feel good and more connected, safe, calm, understood, or refreshed, remember to keep it in your back pocket for when a similar situation arises, or work it into your regular routine.

Creating an environment that promotes my healing made a huge difference on my journey. Instead of just doing healing work in therapy, I am doing healing work consistently every day in different ways depending on my needs, and it doesn't always feel like "work"—play and pleasure are valid needs that also require fulfillment. Healing doesn't always have to be heavy and hard—it can be fun, too. I love cooking and chopping vegetables to promote calmness, and having a dance party with my pets helps me feel energized. Part of healing is also reclaiming your joy, so be sure to make space for activities that make you feel alive.

There's an endless number of paths you could take to heal, and no single way is the 'right' way.

Things That Can Help You Heal

Every now and then I ask my community of trauma survivors on Instagram, "What has been the most helpful for your healing?" I love seeing the unique paths people are taking, and the variety of responses that have come through—from therapy to gardening to community service. If you're looking for inspiration on things that might help you heal that you can investigate further, I've consolidated these suggestions from the community:

THERAPY & TREATMENTS

- Eye Movement Desensitization and Reprocessing (EMDR)
- Cognitive Behavioral Therapy (CBT)
- Cognitive Processing Therapy (CPT)
- Dialectical Behavioral Therapy (DBT)
- Internal Family Systems Therapy (IFS)
- NeuroAffective Relational Model Therapy (NARM)
- Accelerated Resolution Therapy (ART)
- Emotion-Focused Therapy (EFT)
- Exposure Therapy
- Somatic Therapy
- Brainspotting (BSP)
- Ketamine Treatment

DAILY PRACTICES

- Mindfulness
- Meditation
- Breathwork
- Gratitude
- Grounding
- Journaling
- Self-reflection
- Self-compassion
- Yoga

CONNECTION

- Friends and family
- Group support
- Community
- Nature
- Animals and pets
- Spirituality
- Volunteering and community service

SELF-CARE

- Rest
- Quiet time
- Sleep
- Fresh air
- Taking medications (as prescribed)
- Social media breaks
- Crying
- Reading
- Baths and showers
- Exercise
- TV and movies
- Cuddles
- Sobriety

CREATIVITY

- Writing
- Making music
- Making art
- Singing
- Dancing
- Cooking and baking
- Gardening
- DIYs

USING YOUR VOICE

- Sharing your story
- Opening up to loved ones
- Communicating your needs
- Enforcing boundaries
- Advocating for yourself and others

Honor Your Needs as They Evolve with You

When you're healing, you're constantly changing, and different things might help you heal at different points along your journey. Sometimes, we grow out of things that once helped us heal. There may be a certain activity that you did to help you cope with a particularly hard time, and you may feel like you no longer need it, or that you don't need as much of it.

At the beginning of my journey, I was focused heavily on getting my anxiety under control, so I practiced breathwork and mindfulness at least four times a week. Now, I still lean on these tools when I need them, but since I've developed the skills, I don't have to dedicate nearly as much time to practicing. I also used to color nightly and do puzzles for a calming pre-bedtime activity because I was too anxious to follow words on a page, but after my anxiety softened, I slowly returned to reading. When I was having nightmares, I kept a dream journal, but once my nightmares became rare, journaling for that purpose no longer served me.

You can grow out of your therapist too. I started off with a trauma therapist who worked with me on treating my symptoms, and once I felt like I had that under control, I worked with a different therapist who had a more reflective approach and helped me confront inaccurate beliefs I'd held about myself. They were both helpful, each fulfilling different needs. Now I'm no longer in therapy, because at this point on my journey, tapping into my own wisdom has been providing the most value, and I have the skills and relationships in place to handle the challenges life brings my way. But I can guarantee that I'll be back at some point in my life, whenever the stress and pain become too much for me to manage on my own.

My healing journey looks completely different now than it did three years ago, a year ago, and even six months ago. Anything that changes your current situation might change your needs, so it's important to pause every so often to check in with yourself and ask, *What else do I need at this stage of healing? What will help me progress? Am I doing anything that no longer serves me?*

If you notice that you're putting time and effort into something and it isn't providing the same benefits as before, take a break from doing it for a while and see how it feels. (If that something is therapy, I recommend talking about it with your therapist first before calling it quits; it

can be a helpful discussion, even if you decide to stop seeing them.) You can always bring it back into your routine
if you realize you still need it. You're allowed to change
your mind at any point, so don't pressure yourself into
following through with a previous decision if you find it
doesn't fit your needs.

Make your healing choices based on what feels best to you, not what you think you should be doing.

Discovering what helps you heal may feel like a slow
process, and it could take weeks (or months) to determine
what combination of things feel right to you. With some
of the daily practices like mindfulness and breathwork, it
can sometimes take several days of practicing them consistently to see the benefits they bring. Just like physical
strength, these emotional skills take work and consistency
to build.

In a desperate effort to feel better as soon as possible,
you may be tempted to try everything that appeals to you
at once. I recommend taking it one step at a time, one
activity at a time, because if you try several things all at

once, not only will it be overwhelming, but it's harder to determine which activity is making things better. If you try one new activity at a time, you can more easily track how each one affects you. Trying to do several things at once can also make it hard to take action in the first place when it feels like it's too much to handle, or we get so burnt out and depleted early on that we want to give up. Small steps are better than no steps at all, so remember to pace yourself: the activities will be here for you whenever you need them.

When there's a mountain to climb, the journey may feel overwhelming, and you'd give anything for a lift to the top. But unfortunately, there are no shortcuts, and there is no get-healed-quick solution. Even if you have every resource at your fingertips, you can't get to where you want to be unless you're putting the effort into it.

Healing is an internal process, and it only happens when we start showing up for ourselves. On an ever-evolving journey, learning how to do that is an ongoing practice, but each step you take that brings you an inch closer to feeling more at ease, more empowered, or more like your authentic self is an indication that you're healing. Over time, the little steps will add up to miles traveled. Keep going, and one day in the future, you'll look back and see how far you've come.

CHAPTER 6

trauma can't be predicted

It was getting late, around 9:30 P.M.—a rare time to see me out on a Wednesday night in 2017. My client, Joey, had hired me to throw an event at his new restaurant in San Francisco. My friend Andrea was there as my guest, and she and I had made plans to catch up over a glass of wine after the event, but in the end, out of pure laziness, we'd stayed at Joey's restaurant. It was a slow night, so Joey and Ryan, the bartender, had joined us at our table.

Our evening started with discussing marketing ideas on the heated patio, brainstorming how to get people into the restaurant on not-so-busy nights. We'd drunk some nice wine and talked about photography, drones, beer, and a bunch of other things I don't remember. After my third glass of cabernet, I was tipsy. Andrea seemed like she was too, sinking into the booth, relaxed, with a soft smile.

About five minutes before we were planning to leave, Andrea stood up and excused herself to the bathroom. Joey and I continued talking about drones. Then all of a sudden, he got serious. Sitting tall and scanning the restaurant, he interrupted me midsentence to ask, "Where did Ryan go?"

Ryan had gotten up from the table at some point during our conversation, but I assumed he went to the bar. You know, where he worked. He'd been running back and forth from there all night, refilling our wine glasses and bringing us bites to snack on.

"I don't know. He's not behind the bar?" I did a quick 180 to see if he was behind the bar. No Ryan.

Joey was alert. His eyes widened as he asked, "Did he go into the bathroom with her?" Then they got small again as he thought of what could be happening. "Are they hooking up?"

I thought, *What is he even talking about?* I had to set him straight. "No way! Andrea wouldn't do that. And he's married!"

I'd only known Andrea for a year, but I knew she wouldn't hook up with a random dude she'd just met. She was classy and kindhearted, and we usually spent our nights out together *avoiding* men. Ryan also seemed to be obsessed with his wife and daughter, as he had sprinkled stories about them into our conversation throughout the night. I didn't think he'd try to hook up with someone else anywhere, let alone at his place of employment.

Joey abruptly got up from the table, as if he knew something was wrong. He walked to the bathroom and started banging on the door, shouting, "Ryan! Are you in there?"

I turned around to see what was going on. Joey continued banging on the door. "Ryan! Open up NOW!" I thought, *Okay . . . now I'm scared.*

The door opened, and Joey yelled, "What are you doing?! You can't have sex in there!"

Right after he shouted this, Andrea ran out of the bathroom. She didn't have any shoes on—just her blue-and-white-striped dress. With tears running down her face, she cried, "I want to go home! I want to go home!" and made a beeline for the front door.

Ryan and Joey were yelling at each other in front of the bathroom. I didn't want to get in the middle of their fight to go look for her shoes, so I just grabbed her purse and ran out the front door behind her.

As we walked to her apartment, I kept my arm wrapped around her shoulder. She cried so hard that she was nearly breathless. I was shocked. I was clueless. It all happened so fast. I asked her, "What happened? What happened in the bathroom with Ryan?"

Head down, with a shaky voice, she said, "I'm sorry . . . I'm so sorry I ruined your relationship with your client."

I wasn't worried about it because I knew she hadn't done anything to jeopardize the relationship. I told her, "No, you didn't! It's okay. What happened in there?"

With her palms covering her eyes, she cried, "I'm sorry I got you in trouble."

I rubbed her shoulder and tried to get answers from her one last time. "What happened in the bathroom with Ryan?"

She cried, "No . . . I know him."

She wasn't making any sense. Nothing made sense to me. She'd gone from calm and relaxed to crying uncontrollably within five minutes. She'd somehow ended up in the bathroom with Ryan. I questioned myself as I thought, *Did I hear Joey right? Was he yelling at Ryan about having sex in the bathroom?*

We linked arms as we carefully walked up the steps to her building. She was still weepy, but much calmer than she was 10 minutes earlier. She was thankful to be home. I didn't want her to be alone, but I didn't know what I could do if I stayed. She was now safe, in her apartment, and would soon be asleep in her bed. She started looking around her apartment.

I asked her, "Are you going to be okay here?"

"Yeah," she said softly. "What happened to my shoes?"

I was relieved that her shoes seemed to be her biggest concern. She was messed up. *Too much wine,* I thought. I figured she'd feel better after sleeping it off for a while. I hugged her good-bye and said, "Get some sleep. Call me if you need anything."

• • •

The next morning, I found out that Ryan had sexually assaulted Andrea in the bathroom, and when her room-mates took her to urgent care in the middle of the night, they found roofies in her system. Chills rushed through my body as she told me the graphic details of what she could remember, and the guilt immediately sank in.

I had brought her to the restaurant. I'm the one who put her in danger. I was oblivious and didn't know she'd been drugged. I asked myself, *Why did I drink so much?* Maybe I could have been able to tell if I were sober. I felt so stupid for letting someone get drugged and assaulted right in front of me. I didn't pick up on how Ryan, who I'd been around a handful of times, was a predator. I didn't take her home earlier or stay with her longer at her apartment. I didn't call the police or take her to the hospital. I wished I had done more. I wished I could have stopped it. I wished I was a better person, because then maybe none of this would have ever happened.

In the months following, whenever I'd see Andrea, I'd become disgusted with myself, and I'd sink into depression. Even though Andrea told me from day one, "It's not your fault," I believed it was. I thought, *Andrea wouldn't have been assaulted if it weren't for me*, and my thoughts took a turn for the worse. I believed Andrea would have been better off without me and started to think everyone else in my life might be too.

I was so ashamed of my involvement in this incident that I didn't want to bring it up in therapy. I was worried my therapist would judge me for being a bad friend or for retaining a client like that. And then, once I finally brought it up after I had a nightmare about Ryan attacking me, I didn't let my guilt show. My therapist even told me then, "It's not your fault," but still, I worried that if we talked about my guilt, I'd convince her that it was my fault and so I hid my guilt from her until she was able to pull it out of me three months later.

You don't have the magical powers to predict when something traumatic will happen.

During a therapy session a few nights after I had another nightmare about Ryan, we discussed what had happened at the restaurant that night. My therapist gave me a look, indicating that she knew I was hiding something. I let out a big sigh and told her, "I feel guilty. What happened was all my fault."

She asked, "What do you mean it's your fault?"

"She wouldn't have been in the restaurant if it weren't for me. I brought her there. I could have stopped what happened to her." I looked down at my notebook on my lap, avoiding eye contact.

She calmly challenged me. "What could you have done differently to stop it? Not invite her to your event?"

My eyes filled with tears. I looked up at her and cried, "I don't know. We could have left to go to another restaurant after the event so she wouldn't have gotten drugged there."

She challenged me, once again. "How could you have known that she was going to be drugged there?"

I shrugged my shoulders and looked down again. After 10 seconds of silence, she continued, "You couldn't have. You thought you were safe. There was no way to know that someone could be drugged or assaulted there."

I searched for other reasons to blame myself. I thought, *If she's right, how could I feel so guilty?* I told her, "I drank too much that night."

Without hesitation, she said, "That's not relevant. Your drinking didn't make him drug and assault her."

I looked up and explained, "But if I were sober, I might have been able to tell that she'd been drugged."

"How would you know not to drink and stay sober? You were enjoying a night with your friend." I shrugged once again. She went on, "Even for a sober person, it can be hard to distinguish whether someone has been drugged or is intoxicated from alcohol."

I nodded, wiping tears away from under my eyes. I started to feel lighter as she tore down the beliefs I'd held for over a year. Then she told me, "What happened was out of your control. You couldn't have stopped it. The only person to blame is the man who drugged her and assaulted her. Not you."

Once my therapist pointed out that I didn't have the magical powers to predict what was going to happen, I understood that I couldn't have possibly stopped it. When she reinforced the fact that my behaviors weren't the problem, I finally believed that Ryan was the only person to blame. Even though I felt like I had begun to heal from this experience, not acknowledging the guilt for so long kept me from truly moving forward.

Punishing yourself for what you didn't know will only hinder your healing.

Self-blame is often a survival response. Growing up, I convinced myself that I was a bad kid, and that if I behaved better, my mom wouldn't have chased after me with a broom. I needed my mom; without my primary caregiver, I'd be alone in the world. Sometimes, we may unconsciously blame ourselves to avoid addressing the trauma we've endured. When we're focused on what we could have done differently, it's easier to overlook how it affected us. Sometimes, we blame ourselves because we make a mistake, and if we hadn't made it, it may not have resulted in trauma. But there can be multiple truths: you can make a huge mistake and still not be to blame for what happened to you. It can also be scary to admit that we have little to no control over terrible things that happen to ourselves and our loved ones, so we may try to convince ourselves that we *were* in control in order to continue living in the world.

Self-blame comes naturally for many of us. It's easy to look at your experiences and list all the things that you could have done differently to avoid certain things from happening. But you can't see into the future, and you can't predict when something terrible is going to happen. Even if there were "red flags," we most often only recognize them in retrospect. At the time of the event, you didn't have all the information that you have now, so it's unfair to blame your past self for something you didn't know.

You may also blame yourself for how you responded during your traumatic experience, and for not doing more to stop it from happening. But you were in survival mode, and our instinctive survival responses (fight, flight, freeze, fawn) are automatic and involuntary. When you're in danger, there's no time for critical thinking—your body just reacts, and it isn't a conscious decision. You are not to blame for your actions, or lack of action, when you were just trying to survive. You did everything you could to keep yourself safe.

Victim-blaming is rampant in our society, so it can be hard for us not to internalize these messages when we constantly see people questioning victims while giving the perpetrators and harm-doers the benefit of the doubt. People often try to point out what the victim did "wrong" that led to the traumatic event—where they were, what they did before, what they were wearing, and the list goes on. One of the hardest truths is that terrible things, whether trauma, injuries, illnesses, or loss, are all part of life, and they're often out of our control, and I believe people victim-blame partly because this truth is hard to sit with. It feels better to live in a world where bad things won't happen to you as long as you behave properly.

To be clear, if you were the victim, *it wasn't your fault.* You are not to blame, no matter what. It doesn't matter what you did before, during, or after your traumatic experience. It doesn't matter how late it was, where you were, who you were with, what you were wearing, or how much you drank. It doesn't matter if you missed the "red flags." It doesn't matter what you could have done differently. No matter what, you did not deserve what happened to you, and the only person to blame is the person who harmed you.

Even if your trauma is the result of an action you took when you were "in control" (for example, my suicide attempt), if you look back at what led to that decision, whether it was another traumatic experience, an underlying illness, or lack of support, opportunities, and resources, you probably weren't solely responsible. Sometimes, trauma is brought on from a genuine accident (car crashes and injuries, for example). No matter what your traumatic experience was, try to show yourself some compassion; you were most likely doing the best you could at the time. Again, you can't predict the future and the outcome of every decision you make and punishing yourself for something that you can't go back and undo isn't going to help you heal.

Depending on your traumatic experience, healing may require you to take responsibility for your mistakes and the harm you caused, and learn to forgive yourself so you can move forward. When I was in deep pain due to my childhood trauma, I ended up hurting others. For a long time, I'd punish myself for my mistakes, which led to overwhelming self-loathing, shame, and suicidality. I thought I *deserved* the trauma I'd endured as an adult because I had mistreated others as a kid (what goes around comes around, or so they say). But as I built a better understanding of myself and what led me to behave that way, I was able to meet myself with compassion, which ultimately led to self-forgiveness. Self-compassion paves the way for accountability, making it less painful to take ownership of our mistakes, learning from them, and making positive changes instead of shaming ourselves into depression. Had I continued punishing myself for the harm I caused, I'd still be suffering, and there's a chance I'd still be passing along pain instead of helping others heal. Self-punishment doesn't solve anything. It isolates you in a prison of shame, obstructing the path toward amends and resolution. When we deprive ourselves of healing, it doesn't serve anyone.

Don't deprive yourself of healing for something you can't go back and change.

It's hard to heal when you're stuck in the storm of self-blame. It can be destructive, leading to depression and coping mechanisms that don't serve the healing process, and when you're so focused on what you could have done differently to prevent your trauma, it keeps you from progressing. Due to the deep shame attached to self-blame, it can be painful to address, but if you continue avoiding it, it'll just keep chipping away at your self-worth, reducing you to your flaws.

Each traumatic experience carries its own complexities, so overcoming self-blame may look different for everyone. To start, spend some time examining your beliefs around why you think you're to blame. Question yourself like my therapist questioned me. *How could you have known that would happen? How would you have known not to do that?* If you still believe that you are to blame due to something you did, try to build a better understanding of yourself. For example, if your trauma was brought on by an addiction you've been struggling with, perhaps it was a way to self-medicate and cope with a difficult time or another traumatic experience. Building a better understanding of yourself often leads to self-compassion, which can melt away the blame and lead to self-forgiveness. Forgive yourself for what you did when you were hurting, when you were at your lowest point, and when you didn't know any better. Forgive yourself for the mistakes you've made. Remember, you weren't built to know everything; everyone is imperfect, and we all make mistakes.

Working through your self-blame can be brutal, but it's a powerful part of healing. As the blame fades away, you'll gain a new sense of freedom, and you'll be met with less resistance as you continue paving your way.

CHAPTER 7

comparison is a losing game

I had a hard time accepting the fact that Andrea's assault was traumatic to me. Self-blame kept me from bringing it up in therapy for four months, and I also didn't see how that event could have contributed to my PTSD. I thought it didn't matter because it happened to *her*, not me.

When I first started therapy, I couldn't remember my nightmares. I'd wake up breathless, drenched in sweat, heart thumping, on the verge of panic. My anxiety would stick around for the entire day, and when bedtime came, I felt too afraid to sleep. I took sleeping pills to knock myself out (not recommended), and then the cycle would repeat itself. The constant anxiety and sleep issues were unbearable, so I filled my therapist in on what was going on.

She explained, "Sometimes when we don't resolve something when we're awake, our minds will tell us what's bothering us when we're asleep. Your dreams could give us some good information about what's making you anxious."

I was game—I'd do almost anything to find relief. "Okay. How do I remember them?"

Then she asked, "Do you *want* to remember them?" I was taken aback. It was as if she knew my dreams were trauma-related, and I wouldn't like what I would find out.

She suggested that I start a dream journal. Every morning, the second I woke up, I grabbed my notebook and scribbled down every little detail that I remembered from my dreams—I was training my brain to remember them. At first, I could only remember minor details: what I was wearing, who was in it, the type of setting I was in. But as writing in my dream journal became a habit over the next several weeks, I started to remember more.

I had frightening dreams about snakes in our backyard, and men trying to get into my house. I had a dream about my family leaving me behind when we were on vacation in Hawaii. I had several dreams about getting chased, sometimes by an alligator, sometimes by a man, like that morning in San Francisco. Sometimes I was chased by Ryan.

In one of my most terrifying dreams, Ryan snuck into a house I was staying at in wine country by climbing through the bathroom window. He started walking toward me, and I sprinted upstairs into a bedroom and locked the door behind me. Praying someone would hear me outside, I screamed out the window, "HELP! HE'S A RAPIST! HELP!" Then he kicked in the door. I woke up screaming, and I couldn't stop crying.

Ryan haunted my dreams nearly every week, and I started to notice other disturbing thoughts throughout the day. I didn't feel safe at any restaurants or bars, or even coffee shops—anywhere where men worked and beverages were served. I lost all interest in sex. Once when Adam came up behind me and put his hands around my bare hips, a vision of Ryan doing the same to Andrea immediately struck me, and I began panicking. I had intrusive thoughts about men barging into my house, knocking me unconscious, and raping me. I knew something wasn't right, but still, I didn't believe I had a right to be traumatized by that experience. *It happened to Andrea, not me.*

My therapist explained to me that you don't have to be the person directly experiencing a traumatic event to be affected by it: witnessing, being involved in, or learning of traumatic events vicariously can be just as impactful. While I understood what she was saying, and I logically knew that what happened that night with Andrea contributed to my symptoms, her messaging was still hard to internalize. I just kept thinking about Andrea, comparing my experience to hers. I thought, *If I feel this bad, what Andrea is going through must be so much worse*, and because I didn't want to be self-centered or inconsiderate, I pushed my pain away.

Comparing your wounds to someone else's won't help you heal.

After a year of constantly minimizing and dismissing my feelings associated with Andrea's assault, I had to learn how to let myself feel how I *really* felt. I had to be honest with myself about how the experience impacted me. I had to give myself permission to be affected by it, regardless of how much worse it may have been for Andrea.

The more I thought about it, the more my trauma around this event made sense. Because I was so close to what happened that night, it made me feel like it could have just as easily happened to me. I could have grabbed Andrea's glass and drunk the drug-spiked wine. I could have ended up in the bathroom with Ryan. And since it happened at an upscale farm-to-table restaurant in San Francisco where I knew everyone—not a sleazy club or grimy dive bar with randos—I believed it could happen anywhere with anyone, and I feared that something similar would happen again.

It also happened to my friend, someone I care for. Maybe if it had happened to a stranger who I didn't have an existing emotional connection with, that experience might not have affected me as much. But I saw that Andrea was hurting and terrified. I witnessed her running out of the bathroom crying, and then heard the graphic details of what happened from her face-to-face. Her pain added to my pain. Her fear added to my fear. Sometimes emotions are contagious.

It happened to Andrea, but I was there too, and I didn't begin healing from that experience until I stopped comparing my pain to hers.

Trauma Is Deeply Personal

The word "trauma" gets thrown around a lot, and while many of us use the word to describe a traumatic event, trauma is defined as a person's *emotional response* to the event (American Psychological Association, n.d.). Trauma isn't the event itself; it's our individual response to what happened.

We all experience things in different ways. Just like everyone has different fears, passions, and preferences, each person who goes through a traumatic event will have a unique reaction to it. Two people could go through very similar experiences, and one person may struggle with flashbacks, nightmares, depression, and severe anxiety while the other person walks away from the experience without any trauma symptoms. Being unaffected by a traumatic event doesn't mean they're a stronger or more capable person; they just had a different reaction to the experience.

If you were there that night with Andrea, it might not have impacted you the same way—you don't have the same fears as me, or the same history. Andrea's assault happened after I had already been violated by several men, and after I had gone through other traumatic experiences that stole my sense of safety. And even though those experiences took place years earlier, they influenced how I was affected by what happened with Andrea. Whether we realize it or not, each traumatic event leaves an imprint on us, and they impact how we respond to each experience that follows.

We'll discuss this more in Chapter 9, but as you start opening up to others, some people may invalidate your trauma. They may tell you, "That's not trauma," because it doesn't seem traumatic to *them*. They may say, "It could have been worse," which might be true, but that doesn't mean that what you *did* experience wasn't traumatic. They may have even been through a similar experience that they didn't have any challenges coping with, so they may not be able to see how it could affect someone else in another way—sometimes, people can't see that multiple truths exist.

Trauma is deeply personal, and nobody else is in the position to determine what experiences were and weren't traumatic to you: only *you* are qualified to do that. If someone says that what you went through wasn't "that bad," it can still profoundly affect you. You're the only person who has ever experienced exactly what you've been through, and you're the only person living in your body with your thoughts, feelings, and symptoms. If someone tries to invalidate your trauma or says they "don't agree" that it is trauma, remember that your experience is your truth, and your truth is indisputable. No matter how well someone knows you, nobody will ever know your trauma better than you.

It's Not a Competition

My mom has told me, "If you lived my life in Vietnam, I don't think you would have survived." I believe her. The earliest memory she can recall is when she saw a lot full of dead bodies at the age of four. When the war ended in 1975, her father was sent to a prison operated by the communist government where supporters of the South Vietnam government were tortured, abused, and forced to do manual labor. A few years later, her mother was also sent to prison, and my mom was left to care for her eight younger siblings. They were forced to hand over their land and valuables, and after being robbed, they were left with nothing but the roof over their heads. My mom wanted to be a teacher, but since she came from a family of landowners, that wasn't a possibility under the new communist regime. Her only employment opportunity was to work in a factory, which she did for a short period, but the compensation was nothing close to what she needed to help her family survive. If she didn't beg and plead for food, they may have starved to death.

There was no future for her family in Vietnam, so a few months after her parents returned home, they snuck off to a fishing village in the middle of the night and escaped in a small boat, one not built to take on 10-foot waves in the South China Sea. They spent three days at sea with nothing but the clothes on their backs until they landed on the shores of the island Hainan. For two weeks they begged for food, and depended on the rain for water, then traveled along China's southern shores until they reached Hong Kong. After nearly two years in a refugee camp, they were able to make their way to the United States. It was a long and dangerous journey that they risked their lives for, but it ended up being worth it. "America is heaven compared to Vietnam," she says.

I haven't been through anything close to what my mom has. She's told me on several occasions, "You have a good life compared to me," and it's completely true. Compared to everything my mom has been through, the sum of my traumatic experiences seems insignificant, but her trauma plays a role in my struggles too. Trauma can be passed down from generation to generation, not only through environmental factors (the way traumatized parents raise their children), but also through epigenetic changes (the way genes express themselves) that occur in the biology of the parents (Wolynn, *It Didn't Start with You*, 2017). I was born with my mother's traumatic past encoded within my body, which increased my risk of struggling with depression, anxiety, and PTSD. Still, seeing stories about war, rape, human trafficking, and poverty are proof that what I went through wasn't *that bad*, and for a long time, I told myself that I should be grateful that I haven't been through worse. *I'm lucky, I'm privileged, I shouldn't be hurting over this.* Forcing myself to count my blessings was just another way to mask my true feelings, and it kept me from healing.

You'll always be able to find people who have been through something more tragic, and you'll always come across people who are suffering more than you. This isn't a competition, and your trauma doesn't have to be the most devastating experience out there for it to matter. Even if it could have been worse, it doesn't erase what you went through and the pain you've felt. Pain is pain, and unless you tend to it, it isn't going away.

If you have compassion for others struggling, you may feel like you don't deserve to heal when others out there are hurting more than you. *Everyone* deserves to heal, and if you don't heal your trauma, you aren't going to be in a position to help others who aren't as fortunate as you. If you deprive yourself of healing and your pain is weighing you down, how will you have the capacity to support and advocate for others? You can have compassion for others *and* heal your own trauma—you don't have to choose between one or the other. Support others when you can, but don't neglect your wounds. Your pain matters, and unless you make space for your healing, it'll be a challenge to be there for others.

Your trauma is valid, even if it wasn't 'that bad,' and even if others have had it worse.

Keep Your Eyes on Your Road

As you begin healing, you may notice yourself comparing your healing journey to other people's as well. It may be discouraging to see their social media posts where they appear to be healthy and happy when you can barely get through the day. People may share their progress with you, and if you don't believe you have progressed as much, you may not feel like you're healing fast enough. You may see the treatments they've done or the daily practices they've adopted, and wonder, *Am I doing this wrong?*

Because trauma is deeply personal, healing is deeply personal as well. Traumas shouldn't be compared, and neither should our healing journeys. Everyone is facing different challenges and healing from different experiences. Everyone heals in different ways and at different speeds, and not everyone has access to the same resources and opportunities.

Most of us are just trying to figure things out as we go, doing the best we can with what we have. If your healing journey doesn't look the same as someone else's, remember that it doesn't mean you're on the wrong path. While it might be helpful to learn about other people's healing and what's worked for them, remember that their way isn't the only way to heal. They're making choices based on their experiences, intentions, and needs—not yours—so don't doubt yourself if healing looks different for you. When you're so focused on what others are doing, it can distract you from your own journey and waste valuable emotional energy that would be better spent on your own healing.

When we compare ourselves to others, we're setting ourselves up to feel like we aren't good enough, or we aren't doing something right. A lot of times when we see people sharing about their lives, we only see the outcome of their accomplishments. I've been guilty of this too; it's hard to be vulnerable all the time, and it doesn't always feel safe. When people talk about their healing, we often only see where they are now, and don't always see how they got there, all that they've struggled through, or the resources that helped them along the way. We often judge and criticize ourselves for not being better, or for "falling behind," but it's unfair to measure ourselves up against others who are in completely different positions. The self-judgment that comes along with comparing ourselves to others only leads to more internal struggles that often delay the healing process.

While comparing ourselves to others can be harmful, self-comparison can be helpful. Self-comparison helps determine what's most beneficial for your healing, as you notice how certain activities or people affect your mood, symptoms, and how you feel in your body. Comparing

where you were at the beginning of your healing journey to where you are several months, or years, into it will
showcase how far you've come, and continue fueling your
progress. Self-comparison can help create a clearer road
map for your healing, and motivate you to keep moving
forward, so if you're going to be comparing yourself to
anyone on this journey, make sure it's you.

CHAPTER 8

you are enough

For as long as I can remember, people have been trying to force me into boxes and dictate what I am and what I'm not. As an ethnically ambiguous mixed person, people have asked me, "What are you?" before asking for my name. I've been told, "You're not *really* Asian" by friends and colleagues who'd poke fun at my culture. They told me I wasn't a "real" Vietnamese person because they couldn't "see it," and because I only knew a couple of words in Vietnamese (even though not knowing a single word in Czech didn't make me any less Czechoslovakian). People constantly invalidated my identity, so I never felt Vietnamese enough, while the microaggressions and racism I experienced reinforced that I wasn't white enough either. At a young age, through experiences with classmates, I learned that my culture was uncool and that my favorite snacks were "weird" and "gross." By witnessing condescending white ladies talk to my mom, I learned that she was inferior, and so was I. People I'd just met would casually say racial slurs to my face, oblivious to the fact that their words had stabbed me in the heart. Even when you hold great privilege and can "pass" as white, in America, half-white isn't white enough.

I believed that my worthiness was limited to what I accomplished and what I looked like. My parents wanted me to be successful, (physically) healthy, and beautiful, but I could never live up to their standards. They criticized me for almost everything: the way I spoke and ate, my performance in sports, my posture, my weight, and my grades. My mom once told me after receiving a sixth-grade report card, mostly filled with Bs, "If it's not an A, it's an F." Anything less than an A was unacceptable, and because my older sister was a 4.0 student, I was expected to perform at the same level. But compared to my sister, I was dumb, and throughout my academic life, I was never smart enough.

I was "big," "overweight," and "out of shape" as a kid. I had a PE teacher who gave me a nickname, and when he'd refer to me as "Miss Piggy," it gave my classmates permission to do the same. They also called me Francine, as in the cartoon monkey from the TV show *Arthur* that they said I looked like. At first, I laughed along with them because that was easier than admitting I was hurt, but then I bottled up my anger and threw it back at classmates, calling them names they didn't deserve.

My mom and aunties would often tell me, "Lose 10 pounds and you'll be beautiful." I wasn't beautiful as is, but I already knew that based on the girls I'd see on TV, in magazines, and by comparing myself to my classmates that all the boys had crushes on. Even when I'd lost 10 pounds, then another 10, then another by denying myself food and working out excessively, I still wasn't beautiful enough.

When I got to college, I sought validation from men, because if they wanted to sleep with me, that meant that I was desirable and attractive enough. Then my friend called me a slut (not in a fun, joking way) after hooking up with two people in the same week, and I was ashamed.

I had also mentioned that a guy gave me $30 to cover the cab back to the dorm, which I thought was nice, but she laughed as she said, "So he paid you, like a prostitute." I was dirty and trashy—not a respectable person, not classy enough.

Dozens of other experiences that took place throughout my life instilled the belief that I wasn't enough. Most people can relate to this feeling to some extent, as our society is heavily focused on productivity, accomplishments, and being "the best" while providing a very narrow definition of what beauty and success are and what being a good person is. Part of healing for so many of us is unlearning a lifetime of patriarchal lies. But when the shame of not living up to societal expectations compounds with trauma, it often takes an even greater toll on your self-esteem.

When I thought about how I could have prevented my traumatic experiences from happening, I concluded that I was the problem. If I was a better kid, my mom wouldn't have tried to discipline me in that way. If I didn't dance with the random guy on spring break, and if I weren't such a slut, he wouldn't have assaulted me. If I had been more aware of my surroundings on my way to the farmers' market, I would have noticed that I was being followed earlier, and could have made my way to a safe location. If I had stayed sober and knew what being roofied looked like, Andrea wouldn't have been assaulted. *I* was the issue, and soon, I began interpreting everything through the lens of that belief.

I only saw my flaws—with my body, at work, and within my relationships. I dissected every interaction I had and recalled experiences from my past that reinforced the fact that I wasn't enough, and because I was damaged, I would most likely never be enough. I was highly critical and cruel, calling myself a "dumb bitch" and telling myself things like, *I can't do anything right. Ever. Nobody likes me, and I don't blame them.* I didn't have an ounce of confidence in myself.

Viewing your mental health challenges as a weakness can also add to the negative beliefs about yourself, making matters worse. I thought about taking my life again, not too long after I was diagnosed with PTSD. I believed that I was weak for struggling, because again, what I went through wasn't *that bad.* I could barely function, and my responsibilities felt like too much to handle; I wished I could leave it all behind and evaporate into thin air.

Viewing myself through this negative lens turned into a vicious cycle of self-criticism that led me to feel worthless, and it obstructed my healing.

Notice Your Inner Critic

It can be easy to fall back into this cycle. When I'm criticized on social media for not getting a post quite right, or for making a mistake, my thoughts begin spiraling, and my inner critic comes out with a megaphone, telling me that I'm stupid. My critic will go back in time and dig up old memories of all the times that I messed up, further proving the point that I am incompetent. And while I do want to hold myself accountable and grow, when I'm being bombarded with my own harsh criticism, I don't want to get up and try to improve—I want to shut down and hide. This cycle impacts each piece of my life, especially my healing. If you're hard on yourself day after day, it isn't going to support your healing—it's going to sabotage it.

Breaking the cycle of self-criticism is a practice, and if you've carried your self-criticizing habits for most of your life, letting them go isn't going to come easily. Working toward understanding your inner critic will make it possible to continue moving forward on your healing journey when you slip up, make a mistake, or go through a challenging time. There have been times where I've felt triggered and my inner critic has come to attack. Noticing what's happening has allowed me to stop panic in its tracks. Learning to meet yourself with compassion will also provide you with the encouragement to keep trying and not give up.

Start by becoming aware of your negative self-talk. What led to it? Was it triggered by something internal, or something someone else did or said? Notice the language you use with yourself and your tone. Does it remind you of someone who criticized you in the past? My inner critic is judgmental and often sounds like my mom, but meaner, and she curses. Making the connection between your inner critic and a voice from your past can be helpful for some people. Noticing that my critic is mirroring messages I've internalized in the past has allowed me to cultivate self-compassion, as it helps me make sense of why I'm so hard on myself. If it doesn't come up naturally for you, that's okay. But the better the understanding you have of your inner critic, the better position you will be in to comfort yourself when they attack.

Be Nice to Yourself

When I started becoming more aware of my negative self-talk after a mistake I had made at work, I shared my notes with my therapist. She then asked, "How would you feel if Adam or a friend spoke to you the way you're speaking to yourself?"

That question struck a chord in me; I'd never thought of it that way. I clearly don't want to be around anyone who insults me and continuously reminds me of all my flaws, and at that moment, I realized I was the only person in my life who treated me so badly.

I told her that I'd feel terrible, and I'd want to end the relationship. She then continued, "When you're critical of yourself, it can help to pretend like you're speaking to a friend who is experiencing what you're going through instead. We're usually much kinder to friends than we are to ourselves."

As they say, we are our own worst critics.

Our inner critics don't view things from an objective point of view—they exist to remind us that we aren't enough. They're only telling one side of the story, and it isn't the whole truth. Cultivating supportive self-talk (even if we pretend it's coming from a caring friend) can help shape an inner dialogue that's closer to what's happening in reality. While we can still acknowledge our mistakes and take note of where there is room for improvement, comforting yourself with kind self-talk will help you continue moving forward instead of feeding your insecurities and ultimately shutting down.

First, acknowledge what you're going through and notice the feelings that are coming up for you. Maybe you made a mistake, and you're feeling worried, insecure, or remorseful. If you were punished or shamed for that mistake, you might also feel humiliated and hurt. Whatever you're feeling, name it. Try your best to avoid judgment (i.e., *I feel stupid. I'm a failure.*) and to remain observational.

Next, validate your feelings and what you're going through. Tell yourself things like, *This is a tough situation. It makes sense why you feel this way.* Talk to yourself like you would when comforting a friend who is going through the same thing. *Everyone makes mistakes—it's part of being human. You're doing your best.* Use kind and comforting language and try to use a gentle and soothing tone.

I found that once I shift my inner dialogue and allow that shift to set in, I'm in a better position to determine ways in which I can do better the next time around. Instead of being swept into the self-destructive cycle of tearing myself down, which ultimately leads to panic or depression, I'm calmer and can see a path forward. Once I got in the habit of talking to myself in a more caring way while still acknowledging my full humanity, flaws and all, it felt like I had a stronger foundation for my healing. Even on the worst days when a crisis would appear and jolt me like an earthquake, I could comfort myself and withstand the shaking.

Learning how to comfort yourself takes practice and consistency. You may feel awkward and uncomfortable if the only voice in your head up until that point has been critical. Your inner critic may never disappear, but as you continue meeting yourself with compassion, caring self-talk will start to infuse your mind and provide you with much-needed support on your healing journey.

Give Yourself a Pep Talk

If you feel like you're lying to yourself in a way by showing yourself care and support, I get it. When I first started trying to be nicer to myself, I felt like I was forcing my positive self-talk, and in a way, I was, because it was so foreign to me. While I believe learning to validate and comfort yourself is an important skill—a way not to depend constantly on external validation—there's something else you can try to get the ball rolling: create a pep talk folder.

When I was 24 and worked in corporate marketing, I was denied a promotion I had worked incredibly hard for. They recognized my passion, the quality of my work, and the results I delivered, but I wasn't given a clear explanation for why I wasn't promoted. I met the goals they had set, but then they kept moving the target further away. I thought I had proven myself, but they said it still wasn't enough, and the limited self-esteem I had disappeared. Even when my boss praised me, I told myself, *If she really believed that, she would have pushed for my promotion.* I liked the work, and the company was cool, so even though I felt undervalued, I stuck around.

A couple of months later, a campaign I'd managed had come to an end. As usual, I prepared a program recap and sent it off to my boss, who then shared it with the rest of the marketing team. Besides the "beautiful work!" from my boss, I wasn't expecting any recognition. But then I received an e-mail from a VP, copying all the company executives. My eyes filled with tears as I read the ending, which said, "You're a great asset to the company and the team."

I'd never received an e-mail that made me feel so appreciated. I wanted to hold on to that feeling, so I took a screenshot of the e-mail and kept it on my desktop so I could reread it when I was having a rough day—it was hard evidence that I was a valuable member of the team. I started noticing other e-mails with good feedback, so I started taking screenshots of those too, and collected them in a folder I named "Pep Talk." Whenever I felt like I was worthless, I could reread the e-mails, and it softened my feelings of self-doubt. Keeping this folder helped raise my self-esteem so that the next time I didn't get the promotion,

I had enough confidence to realize that I deserved better. Then I quit to start my own marketing business.

Create your own pep talk folder that you can revisit when you feel like you aren't enough. For work, start a folder in your inbox or on your desktop and save any e-mails that make you feel good in there. Take screenshots of encouraging texts from friends and sweet messages from people on social media, and add them to a photo album on your phone so you can swipe through them if you need a pick-me-up. If someone tells you something reassuring in person or on the phone, repeat it to your-self afterward, or write it down, so you don't forget it. If you feel as if you aren't receiving enough encouragement organically, don't be afraid to reach out to a friend and tell them whatever negative thought you're having about yourself: they'll most likely prove you wrong.

You can also start a pep talk folder on social media filled with posts that help you feel seen, ones that melt away your shame, or help you feel good about yourself. Even though I don't know many of the people posting personally, there are so many encouraging creators and communities whose content helps tear down the nega-tive beliefs that I've held about myself for most of my life. I save posts from mixed communities and Asian influ-encers who validate my existence and remind me that my culture and identity ought to be carried with pride. I save posts by people who remind me that all types of bodies are beautiful. I save posts that remind me that it's okay to mess up, and that there is no such thing as being a perfect human because perfection doesn't exist. And when my insecurities begin creeping in, I swipe through them, and remember that whatever I'm going through is part of the human experience—and that being fully human is enough.

You are enough, even as a work-in-progress.

Feeling like you aren't enough can add an additional layer of stress to your healing journey—increasing pressure, making you feel like you need to perform better or do more. And in a world that continuously sends the message that we aren't enough, we constantly have to remind ourselves that we *are*. We do not exist to live up to someone else's expectations or to fit into someone else's mold. Our purpose is not to make other people comfortable, especially if that means leaving parts of ourselves behind. We weren't meant to be good at everything or to be everything to everyone. We do not exist to be flawless.

You are enough, even when you make mistakes, and even when you know you can do better. You are enough, even when you're struggling and need help. You are enough, even when you face rejection and other people tell you that you aren't. While we can all grow, you do not have to strive to become more valid, more worthy, or to prove yourself further; being yourself is already enough, and if anyone tells you otherwise, remember that their opinions and expectations don't define you.

People won't always want you to be your authentic self. They want you to be who *they* need you to be. Healing isn't about pleasing others or being perfect—it's about allowing yourself to be fully human and becoming someone that feels true to you. Once you relieve yourself from the pressure of needing to fit a certain mold, it'll create the space for you to discover what's best for you.

You are enough—always have been.

CHAPTER 9

isolation isn't the answer

When I started experiencing severe anxiety, depression, nightmares, and other trauma symptoms, I just wanted to hide. Although my therapist told me on several occasions, "These are normal responses to terrible events. There is nothing to be ashamed of," I *was* ashamed, and I was in denial.

For several weeks following my PTSD diagnosis, I was secretly hoping that my therapist (and psychiatrist) had made a mistake. I didn't believe that I had a right to be traumatized because my traumas weren't "that bad." I also saw my diagnosis as a personal flaw that made me less worthy, so I rejected it as my reality, and kept my trauma a secret from almost everyone, including my friends and family.

When I finally started telling my friends about what was going on with me, I played down my symptoms, pretending like they weren't a big deal. I told them about how I had anxiety and nightmares, but I didn't mention they were so severe that I wasn't able to work for days, or that I was on the verge of panic when I met them for dinner in San Francisco. I made it seem like trauma hadn't affected my life because I desperately wanted that to be my truth.

I thought I'd feel more loved and accepted by concealing my suffering, but instead, I felt like an outcast.

I wish I'd been more vulnerable. Because I didn't reveal how overwhelming dealing with trauma was, the people closest to me couldn't understand how it affected my life. Because I isolated myself, they couldn't provide me with the comfort and encouragement that I wanted and needed. By not allowing myself to be seen, I didn't give my loved ones an opportunity to be there for me.

Those who give you permission to fall apart are good for your healing.

I thought it would've been the worst possible thing if anyone knew the truth. I was worried my clients would fire me because I didn't think they'd want someone with my condition working on their business. I thought my friends and sisters would judge and gossip about me, and I was afraid my parents would see me as a failure. But my biggest fear was that people wouldn't even care about my pain, which would indicate that I didn't mean much to them at all.

It was unfair of me to make these assumptions; I was projecting my insecurities onto them. Once I started opening up, I found that most of my fears didn't turn out to be true.

It's your right to keep whatever secrets you wish, but take it from me—it feels *so* much better to no longer be hiding. It was exhausting masquerading as someone who was thriving when I was barely getting by. Plus, I can now be honest with people about why I might behave a certain way. Friends and family understand why I sometimes jump in the air and scream when I hear a loud noise, why I want company when I'm traveling on foot, or why it's hard for me to relax and enjoy my cocktail after seeing a creepy man hitting on someone at a bar. I would have been so much more comfortable if I had been more honest earlier.

On your healing journey, there will be times that are more challenging than others, and when you're going through a rough patch that feels overwhelming, connecting with someone compassionate can bring so much comfort. Whenever I'm feeling hypervigilant or depressed, talking to someone, whether in person, on the phone, or online, always makes me feel better. When I'm engaging with another person, I'm forced to be present, in the moment, so my mind can't run off with frightening fantasies. Connecting helps me become calmer.

I know it seems like everyone is always busy, but there are people who will be there for you if you want them to be. Again, it doesn't make you a burden or "too needy": life brings so many challenges, and every single person needs extra support at some point in their life. If it would be helpful for someone to check in with you every once in a while, just so you know that they're "there," see if they might do that for you. If you're not supposed to drink while on your medication, ask them to keep you in check.

If you need someone to help talk you down from panic, ask if it's okay to call them if a situation arises. Your loved ones will want to help you when you're struggling, but they can't read your mind, and they won't know you need support unless you let them know.

The longer I avoided sharing about my trauma, the harder it became to start talking about it. I kept asking myself, *What if this goes terribly? What if they don't understand? What if they abandon me?*, and my anxiety would scare me out of speaking up. But I should have also been asking myself, *What if this goes well?* These burdensome conversations ultimately made me feel closer to my loved ones, strengthening the relationships I cherished most. I found the ones who wouldn't judge or try to fix me when I fell apart but would help me back up once I was ready. I received confirmation that I am loved and cared for no matter what.

I know it can be stressful anticipating these initial conversations, but once you begin opening up, you'll likely uncover the benefits connection brings too.

Your Trauma, Your Rules

Not everyone needs to know about your trauma, and again, you can keep this as private as you wish. But once you feel ready, it will benefit you and your healing if you have at least one person in your corner.

Start by telling the one person you feel the safest and most comfortable with. Adam was the obvious choice for me, but it could be a best friend, family member, roommate, mentor, or anyone else you trust. Those who have a track record of supporting you may be the easiest people to open up to, and they'll most likely want to be there for you on your healing journey.

If you feel good about how the first conversation goes, consider telling others you're close with. Keep in mind that those you connect with most often may have already noticed that something has been "off" with you lately. Sharing what you're going through may help them understand why your behaviors have changed, and they may even be relieved to know that it's because of trauma and not something they did. But remember, you're not obligated to open up to anyone, and you don't owe anyone your story.

Come Prepared

. When you tell people that you're dealing with trauma, most people will want to know what happened. What you decide to share about your traumatic experience is entirely up to you, and you could always tell them, "I don't want to talk about it right now." But if you do want to fill them in, remember that you don't have to get into the details if it's too triggering to talk about.

Be prepared with a shorter version of the story. When people asked me, "What happened?" I often said, "I don't want to get into the details right now because it's hard for me to talk about, but I ran for my life as a man chased me down the street, and then a year and a half later, I was out with my friend when she was drugged and assaulted." They got an idea of what had happened and knew that I didn't want to go any deeper.

Depending on how comfortable you are with the person, you may want to share more than a brief, high-level overview of what happened. If that's the case, be sure to check with the person you're speaking with to make sure they have the emotional capacity to take in the intensity of what you plan to share. Sometimes people are dealing with a lot of stress or even their own trauma, and hearing details they aren't prepared for could be detrimental to their mental health.

Sharing some information about trauma itself might be helpful, as the people you have these conversations with may have misconceptions about traumatic experiences and how they can impact someone. Most people I know associated flashbacks and other PTSD symptoms with war veterans and weren't aware that experiences like mine could also be traumatic. They also weren't aware that people could be productive and appear "fine" and still suffer from depression and anxiety. Consider telling them about some of your symptoms, so they know how they can be helpful. Education can go a long way, and if they have a basic understanding of trauma and your experience with it, they'll be in a better position to support you.

There Is No "Perfect Time"

If you feel like you aren't ready, don't force yourself to discuss this part of your life with people. But if you feel like you're ready and you're just waiting for the "perfect time," know this: you'll be waiting forever. I noticed with myself that waiting to find the perfect time or place is just another avoidance tactic.

Set aside time to chat with someone one-on-one. If you're planning to talk in person, invite them over for lunch or a glass of wine, or plan to go on a hike together. If you meet at a coffee shop or restaurant, that would be fine too, but busy settings are often distracting; you'll want their full attention. When you're making plans, drop the hint that you want to talk to them about something, telling them, "I have a lot to update you on" or "I need to fill you in on something." That way, if it's too hard to start the conversation yourself, they'll likely ask, "What's been going on?" or "What did you want to update me on?" Then you can jump into it.

Unless it's part of your profession, the chances of trauma coming up organically in a conversation are relatively low, and even if it does, you may be caught off-guard and not feel prepared to share what you'd like to. It'll be in your best interest to make the first move; create the space for the conversation and invite them in.

The Message Is More Important

About eight months after I was diagnosed with PTSD, my anxiety intensified as I thought about how I would tell my parents and sisters about my condition as I was getting ready for a family holiday trip. We were going to be sharing a condo for two weeks. Because I always got triggered whenever I slept anywhere outside of my house, I wanted to let them know so they'd better understand my symptoms and wouldn't try to fix me or give me a hard time if my panic started surfacing. Plus, I knew I wouldn't be able to relax on my vacation if I was still working to keep a secret.

For months, I tried to tell my family in person. We'd get together every couple of weeks for lunch, but I could never find the courage to switch the conversation topic from work and travel plans to PTSD. Whenever the time came, my anxiety would surge when thinking about bringing it up, and I'd end up not talking at all. I'd spend most of the time cuddling with the dog on the couch, avoiding everyone.

I thought that the "right" way to share the news with people close to me was face-to-face. I had never been a big fan of phone calls or Facetime, and e-mail felt too impersonal. Still, after several failed attempts, it became clear that I wasn't comfortable enough to discuss the matter with my family in person.

I brought up my dilemma in therapy and talked through a few options with my therapist. She asked how I'd feel about telling them over the phone. Just imagining how that conversion would play out made my heart race. Nine months earlier, when I had just started therapy, my parents somehow found out about it and called me out of the blue on speakerphone with questions. I felt like I was being judged and attacked, and I felt terrible afterward, so I wasn't interested in a follow-up call.

I asked my therapist, "Would it be terrible if I just sent them an e-mail? I think it'll be easier for me to write to them."

She smiled as she softly told me, "Not at all. It may be easier for them to read too."

Right after that appointment, I raced home and started to type, "Dear family." Tears ran down my cheeks as I continued writing, "I apologize for not being able to tell you in person as it is still very hard for me to talk about . . . I will be happy to answer any questions when I am feeling up to it." I went on to tell them how I was diagnosed with PTSD and a brief summary of the most recent traumas I experienced in San Francisco that led to it. I told them about my symptoms and how therapy was softening them. I also included links to articles about trauma, so if they were interested in learning more, they could educate themselves.

After I clicked send, I hugged Adam and started crying uncontrollably. Partly because I felt an immediate release by letting my secret out, but mostly because I was terrified that they would reject me, ignore the e-mail, or not acknowledge my experiences.

Forty-five minutes later, my dad responded, saying, "Thanks for sharing. I read it to Mom. We love you and are proud of how you're dealing with this!" The next morning, my sister replied, saying something similar. I was relieved.

Sending an e-mail wasn't how I imagined sharing the news with my family, but it served its purpose: they learned that I was dealing with the aftermath of trauma, and I found relief. And although my PTSD symptoms ended up being minimal on our holiday trip, a few months later, when I had a panic attack at a bachelorette party in Las Vegas, my sisters were there to comfort me and help me feel calmer. That experience would have been so much more stressful if they weren't already aware of my trauma.

Don't let your preconceptions of the "right way" to share what you're going through hold you back from opening up to people. Remember, you're telling them for you and *your* healing process, so if you can't bring yourself to have a face-to-face conversation with someone, it's okay. Whether it's e-mail, phone call, or text, use whichever medium you feel the most comfortable using. No matter how you choose to communicate, at the end of the day, what's important is that you let them know, so you can get the support you need.

Finding Your People Can Take Time

One evening when I was having dinner with a friend, I shared the story about how I was chased, and her response was, "That's not *that* bad. It could have been worse."

She wasn't wrong. The guy didn't attack me, and I didn't get physically hurt. But she failed to acknowledge how traumatic what I *did* experience was. And when I told her about the series of panic attacks that led to my diagnosis, she said, "I have them all the time"—once again, dismissing what I'd been through. Although mental health issues weren't new to her (which is one reason why I felt comfortable talking to her), trauma was, and she didn't understand why my "just" getting chased was such a big deal.

I don't believe this friend was trying to make me feel bad, but she did. I think she was trying to look on the bright side by noting how lucky I was to get out of the situation unharmed *physically*. And as my therapist pointed out, "Saying she also has panic attacks could have been an attempt, although a poor one, to connect with you."

You may find yourself in a similar position where those with whom you share your trauma may be shocked, and they don't know what to say. Some might not say much because they need some time to digest the information. Some may blurt out a careless comment or point out what you could have done differently. Some may invalidate your trauma because it doesn't seem "that bad" to them. Although it's hurtful, if someone says something dismissive or insensitive, try to give them the benefit of the doubt. Unless they really are toxic and have a pattern of being rude and disrespectful (in which case, it may be time to reevaluate whether you want them in your life), your friends and family most likely aren't trying to make you feel bad. They just may not be prepared for the conversation and might not know the best way to respond.

You may have a friend or family member who will point out what you could have done differently during the traumatic event. When I told another friend about how I was chased, she said, "You should have walked to a police station when you first noticed him following you!" Not helpful. I told another friend about the night Andrea was drugged and assaulted, and she said, "That's why you should always watch your drinks being poured." I felt like they were blaming me for what happened, since they were, in a way, telling me that it could have been prevented. I was caught off-guard. Before opening up to friends, I had only really discussed trauma with my therapist, who was very empathetic, and I was taken aback when others weren't.

People like to provide unsolicited advice and share how they would have handled the situations you've experienced differently. If you feel like they're blaming you, remember that they don't have a complete understanding of what you've been through. They weren't there. They don't know what it was like in the moment. And even if they did go through something similar, they don't have the same fears or history as you.

Since victim-blaming has become somewhat normalized, people may not be aware that what they say might come across as blaming you for what happened. They may not be aware that by questioning your actions and pointing out what you could have done differently, they're shifting the blame to you. You don't have to do it in the moment, but you may want to let them know that what they said was hurtful, and how it made you feel, so that they can do better in the future.

The truth is, not everyone you reach out to will be able to support your healing. Some people may not be able to hold space for your pain because it's too uncomfortable for them to sit with. Some people may lack the emotional capacity, or they may be preoccupied with the chaos in their own lives. It can be devastating when you work up the courage to put yourself out there just to be let down. If they aren't able to support you, know that it isn't because of you—it's because of their own limitations.

I know that it can feel risky to try again after being let down, but don't let one bad experience (or a few) keep you from getting the support you deserve. Everyone you'll speak with is different, and some people will be more compassionate and reliable than others. It can take some time to find that person to lean on, so don't give up—healing is so much more endurable with someone by your side.

Hold on to the people who help you believe in yourself.

If you aren't ready to open up about your trauma yet, that's okay, but don't isolate yourself. Fear and shame want us to hide and disconnect from others, but when it comes to healing, we need connection to keep moving forward. Sometimes, just being in contact with someone, online or offline, with a familiar face or a kind stranger, can do wonders. Even if you discuss something meaningless, like what you ate for breakfast, it can help you feel grounded, remind you of the simple pleasures in life, and make you feel less alone.

Talking about your struggles is hard, but electing not to talk about it while working through your pain in solitude is so much harder. Once you feel ready, let your loved ones in. When you let those closest to you into your darkness, things will become lighter.

CHAPTER 10

healing is an act of love

Trauma not only affects us—it affects everyone in our lives, even if they don't have a clue what we're going through. After going through a life-altering experience, our views of the world change. Whether we realize it or not, trauma changes the way we present ourselves, and the way we perceive ourselves and others. Trauma changes our relationships and how we engage with people. Sometimes it can feel like you're having a never-ending battle with yourself, and even if it isn't your intention, you might drag your loved ones into the war zone.

I've hurt people when I was in deep pain and struggling to cope. I was the most dangerous to myself and others in middle school and high school when I was irritable and angry, and didn't know why. I was cutting myself, and because I wasn't planning on living, I never thought I'd face the consequences of making fun of people behind their backs and saying mean things to their faces. I picked on others to feel better about myself. I was miserable, and I wanted to bring others down with me, so I'd feel like less of a failure—so I'd feel less alone.

One time, my sister accused me of having a crush on a kid that the whole school thought was weird. I don't remember how she got that idea, but it was untrue. I kept yelling, "Stop saying that! I do not!" but she kept going, saying that it must be true because I was getting so mad. Suddenly, I became full of rage and jammed a pencil into her arm. Being teased and not being heard had triggered me, and even though I knew that what I did was wrong, I couldn't handle my emotions.

I had these outbursts throughout my childhood. I'd scream at my mom and sisters regularly when I felt ganged up on and like nobody was listening to me. We fought and insulted each other far more than we ever supported each other. I remember running to my room after yelling at my family, then slamming a water glass onto the floor. I walked on the shattered glass to my bed, then cried for the rest of the night. I lost many friends after getting into arguments where we were yelling at each other, saying things we didn't mean. I felt like I was destroying my life, but I didn't know how to make it stop. I wanted a way out.

I hated who I was, and after high school graduation, I saw an opportunity to reinvent myself. I went to a college across the country that nobody in California had ever heard of, feeling relieved that I could start over and become the nice, fun, smart person that I thought everyone would like. I was a new person. But still, I buried my pain, and while I tried not to harm myself or others (at least not intentionally), through my excessive drinking and reckless behavior, I continued harming myself.

Struggling with trauma gives you every right to be upset, angry, or afraid, but it doesn't give you a right to harm others.

I got married seven months before I was diagnosed with PTSD. Adam and I had been together for four years before our wedding, and we *never* fought. It was unreal; I had never gotten along with another human so well. I knew he was my person for this reason, and because he was the first person in my life who I felt like I could truly be myself around. While I'd been dealing with anxiety and nightmares for years before my diagnosis, our relationship changed once the panic and other symptoms appeared in full force.

Adam was incredibly supportive throughout the process; he helped me find a therapist and comforted me when I woke up crying in the middle of the night. But because I was exhausted and on edge, my patience was limited, so I'd snap at him. If he did something that even *slightly* annoyed me, I'd say something passive-aggressive

to shame him, so he'd stop. I'd criticize him and start arguments over trivial things, like how he used a hand towel to
dry dishes. When he wouldn't listen to me because he was
distracted watching TV, or when he was being dismissive,
I'd yell at him, saying that he *never* listens and doesn't care
about me. It may have felt like that at the moment, but I
knew it was untrue. I was in pain due to my trauma, and I
blamed him for things that would go wrong, just because
he was the only person that was always around. Sometimes it's easier to blame and project our pain onto others
than to admit we feel out of control.

Every day, I'm thankful for his patience. I'm thankful
he knows me well enough to understand that I'm not
myself when I'm hurting, and when I'm heated, I'm not
thinking clearly, and I often don't mean the things I say.
My PTSD made our first year of marriage a challenge,
but over time, I learned how to process my emotions in
healthier ways. I've learned how to take a step back when
I'm feeling overwhelmed, so I don't take it out on Adam
or anyone else around me. And as my symptoms softened and I began feeling better, I naturally started treating others better.

No matter how much pain we're in, and no matter how
hard our lives may be, it's not okay to mistreat others and
continue the cycle of harm. Hurting others is my greatest
regret in life. Since first grade, I was bullied, and I thought
that it was okay to do the same to others. It wasn't. I may
have inflicted trauma onto others, and they may have
passed it on to other people too. This cycle of harm can
also show up in families. My mom disciplined me similarly
to the way her parents disciplined her. I imagine our lives
would have been different if she'd worked toward healing
her wounds, but coming from a war-torn country where

survival was priority, healing was a luxury she couldn't afford. I have compassion for my mom, just like I have compassion for my younger self who didn't know how to handle her pain any better. But now I know that healing ourselves stops the cycle of trauma, and caring for ourselves puts us in the best position to care for others.

Prioritizing your healing isn't selfish—your loved ones will benefit from your healing too.

"

Setting Boundaries

As we previously discussed, healing is an active process, not a passive activity, and the things you're doing to help you heal may turn into a time commitment. It's crucial to protect your time so you have enough space for your healing, not only so you can feel better, but so you can be the best partner, family member, and friend possible. Boundaries allow us to make room for our healing while showing others that we still care.

Even after I began to understand how important it was to prioritize my healing, fear kept me from setting the boundaries I needed to protect my space for that healing. I was worried I'd get fired if I missed a client's call while I was at my therapy appointment, or if I didn't respond to an e-mail that came through at night. I agreed to help friends with social media for their side hustles when I was already at capacity because I didn't want them to be upset with me for letting them know that I wouldn't be able to. I agreed to go out to bars with friends when I was already anxious and tired because I feared they'd stop inviting me, and I didn't want to be left out. Even when I was at my limits, on the verge of panic, I forced myself to go to family gatherings to avoid getting guilt-tripped for not showing. I feared that saying "no" and letting people down would make me unlovable.

Most of my fears were irrational. People don't typically get fired for not responding to an e-mail right away, and friends and family are understanding (most of them, anyway). Once again, I made assumptions, and not being able to express my own needs and set boundaries made me anxious, burnt-out, and resentful. Boundaries are crucial—for your own healing *and* for maintaining healthy relationships with those around you.

Figure Out What You Need, Then Communicate It

The first order of business in setting boundaries is to identify your needs, so you can put parameters in place to protect them. Think about what others do that makes you feel stressed, anxious, depleted, or resentful, then determine what boundaries could be in place to make you feel better about the situation. For example, if anxiety surfaces when you see an e-mail come through at 8:00 P.M. on a

Monday from your boss, stressing you out and making it challenging to relax before bedtime, you need to set a work boundary. If a partner touches you in a way that triggers you, setting a boundary with them so they don't touch you in that way, or having them ask for consent first, would be beneficial.

I loved spending time with Adam, but I also *need* my alone time. I need time to journal or cry or just stare off into space. I need space to read or write in peace, without any distractions. I felt like I was expected to be available to chat with him at all times because he was my spouse, and I was feeling frustrated and resentful when he'd interrupt me. I'd snap at him, asking, "What do you want?" and he would feel hurt because I pushed him away. It only created more tension between us.

It was unfair of me to react that way toward Adam. I never told him that I wanted to be alone in the first place, so he couldn't have known not to interrupt me. Boundaries don't work unless you communicate them. People can't read your mind, so they won't be aware of when they're pressing your limits unless you tell them what they are. I started letting him know when I needed alone time, saying things like, "I'm going to go write for a bit, but we can get together for dinner at 7:00," or "I need some quiet time. I'll come back out to watch TV when I'm ready." Once I let Adam know that I needed space, he'd respect my wishes, and we were both happier.

It can be harder to communicate your boundaries with certain people, like your boss and others you depend on for employment or other central needs. Reasonable bosses should respect a simple boundary like, "I will be available until 6:00 P.M. on weekdays to answer e-mails and calls, but anything after 6:00, I will get to the following morning."

They should understand that you need time away from work to recharge so you can perform the best you can.

Protect Your Peace

You'll most likely run into someone who will violate your boundaries, so be prepared. You may need to continue enforcing your boundaries to make them stick. Sometimes people genuinely forget, or if it's something new for them, there may be an adjustment period as they get used to it.

For example, if your boss doesn't seem to have a personal life and works around the clock, chances are they will still be e-mailing you at all hours. If you feel like they still expect you to be online when they are, you may need to remind them of your boundaries to reinforce what is and isn't appropriate. If you don't feel like they expect you to respond, but seeing their e-mails still bothers you, you can turn off your phone or your notifications. You can have your phone automatically shift into "do not disturb" mode starting at 6:00 P.M., so if you receive an e-mail after hours, you won't get pulled back into work.

If someone continuously violates your boundaries and it's bringing unnecessary chaos to your life and taking an emotional toll on you, you may want to take a step back and reevaluate the relationship.

I had a client who kept trying to get me and my employee to do things that were out of our scope of work— meaning, she wanted us to do extra work for free that we had never agreed to and had no interest in doing. We continuously had to remind her what was in our contact and what we were hired to do, and whenever she requested that we do something outside of our agreement, my anxiety would go through the roof. It became clear that she didn't respect my boundaries when she told me, "I would like you to be more flexible." And when I told her that I would not, she said I was being unreasonable. I knew at that moment that either she was going to end the relationship, or I would. When I got the news that they were terminating our agreement, I felt a huge sense of relief: no longer having someone who continuously disrespected my boundaries made me feel more at peace.

You have a right to have needs, to be treated respectfully, and to say "no" without feeling guilty. Your boundaries should be honored, and if there is anyone in your life who makes you feel like your needs are less important or unreasonable, know that you deserve better.

Your Habits Need Boundaries, Too

In addition to setting boundaries with people, sometimes we need to set boundaries with technology, our devices, and the type of content we consume to conserve our emotional energy.

I love reading memoirs, especially those written by fellow trauma survivors. Reading their powerful stories helps me feel seen, and while there are scenes that are triggering and hard to read, I feel connected to them: they remind me that I'm not alone. I mostly read at night, as it's part of my daily nighttime routine, and often I ignored the fact that some of these books were making me anxious. They also made it hard for me to fall asleep, and sometimes, I'd have nightmares. I knew I'd be better off not reading these books, but I didn't want to stop.

Once I realized that I shouldn't be reading (or watching) any anxiety- or fear-provoking content at night, I didn't stop reading survivor memoirs altogether. Instead, I created some guidelines for myself. Before starting a new book, I read the reviews on Goodreads, as the community there is typically good at providing content warnings so that I know what I'm getting myself into. If it seems like there are parts that might trigger me, I'll wait to read that book during the day or on the weekend, several hours before I start getting ready for bed. Then I plan to watch a comedy, read something light, or play cards with Adam, so I'm not stuck in the world the author created for too long. I do the same thing for triggering TV shows (hello, *Law & Order SVU)* that I enjoy too.

As someone who has worked as a social media consultant for six years, I can tell you that social media was designed to keep us scrolling and keep us coming back to the apps over and over. We can go on Instagram or Twitter to check something super quick, and then the next thing you know, 20 minutes have flown by. It's time-consuming, and can be draining. While social media might help us feel connected, without boundaries, such engagement keeps us from connecting with our loved ones in real life. I can't tell you how many times I've unconsciously tuned Adam out because I was sucked into my Instagram feed. There were a few years where I couldn't take a real social media break due to my work, but once I hired a fantastic employee who made it possible for me to log off over the weekends or on vacation, my life changed. I felt recharged, less anxious, less stressed, more connected, and I felt better about myself.

If scrolling through social media makes you anxious or just puts you in a bad mood (whether that's from comparing yourself to flawless-looking people, seeing triggering content, or coming across mean-spirited comments), you don't need to delete all your accounts and go completely off the grid. Unfollow the pages and people that make you feel bad about yourself and like you aren't enough. Set some limits for yourself, whether it's not allowing yourself to check social media first thing in the morning, limiting the amount of time you spend on social channels each day, or establishing a nightly detox. You can also take social media breaks for a few days, weeks, or however long you need to nourish yourself offline.

Adam and I also have "no phone zones" so we can spend quality time together without our phones distracting us. When we're watching a show together or playing a game of gin rummy or Scrabble, we'll leave our phones in another room, so we aren't tempted to pick them up and start scrolling. I'll often leave my phone zipped up in my purse when I'm out having lunch or dinner with friends, and while I sometimes miss out on taking pictures, I never regret being completely present with them.

If keeping up with politics gets your blood boiling, try to cut back on the time you spend reading or watching the news. For years, I believed I always had to know everything happening in our country and around the world, so I was constantly on the lookout for new juicy stories. But after taking a hiatus, I found that I wasn't missing anything; the most important news always found me through friends, family, or social media. Although I didn't completely cut myself off from the news, no longer searching for it significantly improved my mental health.

Boundaries like this don't have to be all-or-nothing situations: they're responsible compromises. If you know something isn't good for your mental health and is limiting your capacity to heal, it's important to be honest with yourself and recognize how it's affecting you no matter how much you may love it, or think you need it. If you're engaging in any activities that trigger you, or bring on unnecessary stress, start to wean yourself off of them. It may feel hard to let go at first, so it might be helpful to replace the activity with one that's more relaxing (like cooking, painting, reading, or watching a comedy) to distract yourself. After a few weeks, take note of any improvements in your mood; you may find that you no longer need as much of it, or any of it, in your life.

When you invest in your healing, everyone receives the dividends.

When we're hurting, we may take our anger and pain out on others, causing more pain. When we're hurting, we may unintentionally hurt people by being distant, or ghosting them, sending the message that we don't care for them, and they don't matter. When we're hurting, whether we mean to or not, we often push others away, but as we discussed in the last chapter, we need our relationships to keep healing.

When our symptoms are no longer consuming us, we have the breathing room to be patient and caring. When we're feeling better, we're typically kinder to others (and ourselves). When we're no longer on edge and constantly overwhelmed, it's easier to connect with others more deeply, instead of pushing them away. When we're feeling more grounded, we're in a better position to be there for others.

Healing is a powerful force. When you heal, your loved ones, communities, colleagues, and even strangers you interact with feel the benefits too. Give yourself the love you deserve by creating space for your healing, then let it flow to the rest of the world.

CHAPTER 11

hold space for the goodness

I used to love San Francisco. I loved urban hikes and picnics in the park. I loved the neighborhood café and the charming ring from cable cars as they passed by. I loved the farmers' market and exploring the city carefree. But after getting chased, that all changed.

I no longer felt safe in San Francisco. That experience was proof that something terrible can happen, even when you're in an area where you've always felt safe. Andrea's assault took place 18 months later and further supported this hypothesis. But it wasn't just San Francisco. The world felt dangerous to me. No matter where I was, I constantly scanned my surroundings for danger, watching (and listening) closely for any red flags. Even in my own home, I didn't feel safe enough to let myself relax. I feared that something terrible might happen to me (or a loved one) again, so I always prepared myself for the worst. Eventually, I could only see the potential for bad things to happen, no matter the situation.

Whenever I'd catch a man staring at my body, I'd think, *He's going to attack me*, and I'd rush to get out of sight as soon as possible. When I'd receive a passive-aggressive e-mail from a client, I'd think, *She hates my work.*

She's going to fire me. I'm going to go out of business! When I saw two friends got together for lunch without me, I thought, *They hate me. They're probably talking shit about me.* If Adam didn't return my call when he was on a business trip, I jumped to the worst conclusion: *He's cheating on me.* I'd take one small piece of information and blow things out of proportion.

It was exhausting having these thoughts—it would make my anxiety spike and stress levels rise, but I couldn't help myself. Because I'd been preparing myself for the worst-case scenario for years, it was like I trained my brain only to anticipate negative outcomes, and it was impossible to entertain any other possibilities until I was proven wrong.

Trauma can trick you into thinking that good things in your life don't exist.

Catastrophic thinking is common for those of us who've experienced trauma; we know first-hand that terrible things can happen, and to protect ourselves from disaster happening again, we prepare ourselves for the worst potential outcome. But constantly preparing for danger has consequences. Over time, we can develop negative thinking patterns that have the capacity to impact every area of our lives, ultimately leading to depression (Anchor, 2010).

Before my PTSD symptoms surfaced, I saw the world from a more neutral point of view. I'd be able to identify the pros in addition to the cons in most situations, and sometimes, I was optimistic. I had things to look forward to, and there were times when I was hopeful about the future. Even though my inner critic has always had a strong voice, there were moments when I was able to find the good in myself. That all changed when I became over-whelmed with my trauma, and I started to hold a negative bias. It was like I had tunnel vision, focusing on the nega-tives in my life and what could go wrong when there was so much good along my peripherals.

One afternoon, I looked at a picture sitting on my console table from our honeymoon ten months earlier. I thought to myself, *I miss that,* and tears began running down my cheeks, because that trip was the last time I could remember being happy. I hadn't realized how unhappy and hopeless I felt until I was reminded of how I felt before. It wasn't like I woke up and suddenly felt differ-ent; my mood shifted little by little over time. Sometimes depression sneaks up on you like that.

Notice the Goodness That Already Exists

When I explained my concerns around my constant negativity and mood changes to my therapist, she told me, "That makes sense. Trauma has that effect on people. This is something you can easily work on if you'd like to."

She suggested that before I go to bed each night, I make a list of five good things that happened earlier that day. She explained, "It challenges you to notice the good things in your life. If you keep at it, you'll eventually train your brain to find the positives instead of just focusing on the negatives."

Later that evening, I sat down with my notebook and searched my memories for anything noteworthy that happed earlier in the day. It was just an ordinary day made up of e-mails, basic meals, therapy, and household chores. Nothing stood out. After about ten minutes of doodling in the margins, I realized that in order to complete the exercise, things that are part of my daily routine would have to make it on the list. Because, realistically speaking, most days are mundane, and if it takes something extraordinary to happen to qualify as a "good thing," then coming across anything worthy of listing would be a rare occurrence.

With this new insight, I reexamined my day, trying to notice the good in the little things that took place. I had a slow start to my morning, sipping coffee with Adam on our couch. I thought, *That was nice, I guess*, and scribbled it down as number one. Going on a walk in the neighborhood, going to therapy, cooking dinner, and making my kitchen spotless made up the rest of my list.

When I did the same exercise the next few evenings, I included some of the same things, and I also noticed other little things that were good in my life. Catching up with a friend I hadn't spoken to in weeks, giggling as we reminisced about our past adventures. Cuddling on the couch with Adam, watching *Saturday Night Live*. Getting paid. Making a perfect cup of Vietnamese coffee—strong and sweet. Finishing a book and starting a new one. Discovering new growth on a houseplant. Sipping homemade lemonade in my backyard on a sunny day.

After doing this exercise for a week, finding the good started coming more naturally, and some days, my list grew to seven or eight. I started acknowledging the goodness that was already in my life, bringing more awareness to the simple pleasures that I'd been taking for granted. By noticing and appreciating the little things in life, and my tiny victories, I was infusing my mind with small doses of positivity, and the heaviness I was feeling started to fade away.

After about three weeks of doing this "Five Good Things" exercise, I noticed that I was less anxious and more peaceful. I still thought about the potential for negative outcomes, but more often, I held a neutral, more realistic point of view. I felt less miserable and hopeless. While I still didn't *love* my work, it was no longer unbearable, and I even expanded my business. Adam and I were fighting less, and I felt incredibly grateful to have a supportive partner by my side. I felt less fearful, and after months of avoiding people, I put effort into seeing friends again. I still had plenty of bad days, of course, but instead of thinking that I was doomed, I recognized that even though I was having a hard time, I was going to be okay.

I encourage everyone to give this exercise a try, whether you're struggling with depression or not. Even when I'm feeling my best, I'll take a few minutes each night to acknowledge the goodness in my life, as it grounds me and helps me feel content. When I've had a horrible day, this exercise is often the last thing I want to do, but I always feel better after jotting down some good things, even if I can only list three or four. Before, I'd lie down in bed, anxiously thinking about how I made a mistake, or how a client made me feel undervalued, which made it impossible to fall asleep. Shifting focus onto the good things leading up to bedtime helps me feel calm, priming my brain for a restful night.

Your five good things can be anything that made you smile, fulfilled a need you had, or made your day more pleasant. It could be a tiny victory, whether it's taking a shower, receiving good feedback at work, or reading a chapter of a book. It could be talking to a friend, cuddling with your pet, or watching the sunset. It could be enjoying a meal, expressing your creativity, or singing along to a favorite song. The first few times you try this exercise, you may struggle to find your good things, and it's okay if you can only list two or three. Once you get into the rhythm of bringing awareness to the goodness in your life, you'll start to notice it all around you.

When you reject your emotions, you reject an opportunity to identify parts of yourself that need healing.

I want to be clear: training yourself to identify the positives in your life does not mean that you should push away unwanted emotions—that doesn't serve the healing process. As we discussed in Chapter 3, all emotions, even "negative" ones that are challenging to process, are completely valid, and they can give us good information about ourselves. By rejecting our sadness, loneliness, guilt, anger, and jealousy, we're rejecting an opportunity to identify parts of ourselves that need healing. We should always try to listen to our feelings, and work toward understanding them, instead of burying them; otherwise, they may build beneath the surface and come back stronger, causing more pain. (And in my experience, suppression has also led to depression.) Healing isn't about feeling good or being positive 100 percent of the time: it's about learning to face your challenging emotions with curiosity and compassion, not judgment, and recognizing that you have what it takes to work through them.

Positivity can certainly become toxic when we use it to cover up or minimize our pain. Forced positivity and optimism isn't the goal when you're identifying the good things. Negatives and positives often co-exist, and sometimes when we're overwhelmed with the obstacles in our lives, we lose sight of the goodness that already exists.

Healing is just as much about holding space for the good as it is about working through the pain.

When you're healing, sometimes you can be so focused on holding space for your pain that you forget to hold space for the good stuff too. The little things may seem insignificant at times, but they matter. It's the little things that hold the power to help us feel more joyful, peaceful, and content in our lives. The joy we feel from "big" things (like a vacation or a promotion) is usually temporary, but leaning into the little pockets of goodness that we come across each day can provide comfort that's sustainable.

The next time you notice something that makes you smile, brings you warmth, or helps you feel good about yourself, don't dismiss it. Embrace it. Let it soak in with a deep breath. Let the good feelings travel throughout your body, even if just for a minute. Dealing with trauma is hard enough, and you deserve every bit of goodness that comes your way.

CHAPTER 12

don't downplay your gains

Three months into my healing journey, things finally started to feel like they were getting a little better. While all my PTSD symptoms were still present, I could perform at work and make it through the week. I didn't feel "normal" yet—not even close—but I felt like I finally had some breathing room after spending months in survival mode, just trying to make it through each day.

I was trying so hard, and I was exhausted. I practiced becoming vulnerable and started sharing more with my therapist (but still kept plenty to myself). I was using my coping skills, constantly making observations to better understand my triggers and feelings, while packing as much self-care into my weeks as possible. It was emotionally draining, and the payoff didn't seem like much. For all the effort I was putting into it, I thought that I should've made more progress by then, and I started to lose trust in the process.

In my next therapy session, I spent the first 40 minutes of our 45-minute session complaining about a client and telling her about an argument I had had with Adam. I didn't feel like putting any real effort in, partly because

I was questioning whether therapy was really working for me (once again), and partly because I was wasting time to avoid bringing up the heavier, trauma-related stuff. During a long, awkward silence, I quickly glanced over at the clock and saw there were still four minutes remaining. I couldn't think of anything else to bring up, so I blurted out, "Sometimes I wonder if this is really helping me. Shouldn't I have made more progress by now?"

My therapist smiled as she gently said, "I think you're making a lot more progress than you're giving yourself credit for." When I heard these words, my chest tightened, and I felt like crying but didn't know why. I nodded, swallowing my tears, trying to keep a straight face.

She told me that she'd witnessed it, that she could tell that I was becoming more comfortable in therapy, and that if I spent some time reflecting on it, I'd be able to see my progress too. And then time was up.

I started crying as I was driving home, and I couldn't stop. Early on in my healing journey, I discovered that when I'm anxious or angry or upset or overwhelmed, journaling always helps. Writing whatever comes to my mind, honestly, without rules, without caring about spelling or my handwriting or word choices, always helps me feel better; it releases whatever I'm bottling up and helps me feel calmer. So, once I got home, I dumped my thoughts into my journal.

I wrote about how I felt sad but didn't know why. I wrote about how I felt embarrassed when a woman at the crosswalk caught me singing to SZA's "The Weekend" with tears pouring down my face when I was stopped at a light. I wrote about how I first felt the urge to cry when my therapist told me that I was making progress. I asked myself, *Why is that? That wasn't mean or anything.* After thinking about it for a couple of minutes, I realized that I wasn't crying because I was sad: I was crying because *she believed in me.* And as someone who had a hard time believing in themself, it was hard to sit with words that challenged my own beliefs.

I moved on to reflect on my progress, like my therapist had just suggested. I first thought about what brought me into therapy: the series of panic attacks, nightmares most nights of the week, anxiety so intense that I couldn't work or sleep or relax. I thought about how I felt paranoid and avoided leaving the house. I thought about how I didn't want to see or talk to anyone. I thought about how I didn't know what my triggers were, or what "triggers" even were, and how I cried almost every day but could never identify why.

Then it hit me. *Wait, I just did that!* Then I slowly started listing all the "wins" I'd experienced since I began healing:

- I'm better at identifying my thoughts and feelings

- I've learned how to cope and self-soothe through journaling

- I'm becoming more aware of my triggers

- I have a better understanding of my symptoms

- Practicing deep breathing and mindfulness is starting to come more easily

- I have panic attacks a couple of times a month now, instead of a couple of times a week

- I have nightmares two or three times a week, instead of four or five

- I'm not having as hard of a time falling asleep

- I'm not relying on Xanax as much
- I'm better at remembering my dreams
- I'm opening up in therapy more
- I sometimes feel like I can relax
- I'm no longer running from my past

After 30 minutes of searching for the ways in which I've progressed, I filled up an entire page in my journal. I looked over the list and thought, *I guess that's kind of a lot.* Seeing my progress on paper made it seem more real, but I still resisted giving myself credit because I felt like I didn't deserve it.

Growing up, I thought that only monumental achievements were worth acknowledging and celebrating. I was expected to perform well, so things like getting an A on a test weren't a big deal and didn't call for a celebration. When it came to healing, I felt the same way. My condition was *supposed to* improve; that's what was expected. Feeling better wasn't a big deal, especially when I still had a long way to go.

Later that evening, as I was chopping veggies for dinner, my therapist's words popped into my mind again. I repeated them to myself, and then thought, *Maybe I should try giving myself some credit.*

I reread the list before I went to bed. I told myself, "Yes, I did all that, and it hasn't been easy. *This* is progress. I worked hard for this, and I deserve to feel good about it."

The next day, I felt more content, and already started to feel better about where I was on my healing journey. Doing the simple task of honoring my progress shifted my mindset from *I haven't done enough* to *look at how far I've come*, and it gave me the encouragement to keep going.

Healing is the process of change, not a destination where you are symptom-free.

"

Remind Yourself of How Far You've Come

When you're in the thick of healing, it can be difficult to notice your progress from one week to the next. But if you compare where you were one month, three months, six months, or a year ago, the strides you've made will become so much more obvious.

First, think back to where you were at the beginning of your healing journey. Remember how intense your symptoms were, how frequently you had panic attacks, nightmares, and flashbacks. Think about how well you could identify your feelings, triggers, and limitations. Think about what you were avoiding and how you interacted with people. Think about any unhealthy ways you coped with your trauma and any self-destructive behaviors you used to engage in. If it helps, write everything down in a notebook or in the notes app on your phone, so that you can reference back to it throughout your journey. I have a page in a journal titled "Where I Started" that I sometimes revisit as I'm reflecting.

Next, think about how you feel now (if you just started your healing journey recently, come back to this step in a month or so). Notice how your symptoms have improved. If you started out having nightmares four times a week and now you only have them three times a week, that's a win. If you used to have no idea what your triggers were, and now you've identified a few of them, that's excellent progress. If it used to take you several days to recover from a panic attack and now you can calm yourself down within a day, that's a huge step forward. If you had to take a break from work or school because your symptoms were too intense, and now you're back at it, amazing! If you're starting to be able to soften your anxiety due to any breathing exercises, grounding techniques, or other coping skills you're developing, that's something to be proud of. I suggest jotting these things down as well, since seeing all your wins listed on paper can make your progress clearer and make it seem more real.

Remember the steps you took to make it all happen. Even if you had help along the way, *you* made it possible; nobody else did your healing work for you, and it didn't happen magically on its own. Allow yourself to be proud of these little victories, no matter how small they seem. Every inch of progress adds up to a huge step toward healing, and if you keep reminding yourself of how far you've come, it'll continue to fuel your journey, giving you the motivation to keep moving forward.

If you find yourself downplaying your gains because you don't believe you've come far enough yet, remember that healing is the process, not a destination. Healing involves noticing, learning, practicing, allowing, grieving, connecting, and celebrating, among many other things. If you're putting the effort into healing, you *are* healing. Even if you're trying new things that don't work out, as you begin to understand what works for you and what doesn't, you're healing. Even if you're confused or frustrated with the process, that means you're trying, and if you're trying to find the path forward, you're healing. Healing looks different at different times, and you might be healing even if it doesn't feel like it.

Signs You're Healing

Healing is a slow journey, and sometimes the progress is subtle and not easy to detect. Healing isn't just about experiencing the groundbreaking "aha" moments; more often, it's the little steps we take each day that bring us closer to feeling more at ease, more empowered, or more like ourselves. Healing happens little by little, one small win at a time.

If you're having a hard time identifying your growth as a work-in-progress, here are a few signs I've noticed along my journey that indicate you are healing:

- You've acknowledged what you've been through
- You're starting to get more comfortable allowing yourself to feel however you feel
- You're learning to identify and listen to your feelings
- You're becoming aware of your triggers
- You're noticing how your trauma has affected you
- You're learning how to be more present
- You're learning how to validate your own experiences and feelings

- You're letting go of self-blame
- You're becoming aware of your inner critic
- You're learning to meet yourself with compassion
- You're becoming aware of your limits
- You're learning to identify your needs
- You're learning to honor and communicate your needs
- You're learning to ask for and accept help
- You're developing a better understanding of what you can and can't control
- You're starting to let go of people and things that no longer serve you
- You're forming supportive relationships
- You're learning how to set boundaries
- You're noticing who and what helps you heal
- You're creating space for joy
- You're practicing vulnerability
- You're starting to look back on your past with less judgment or shame
- You're starting to realize you're so much more than what happened to you
- You're starting to realize that what happened to you matters
- You're starting to realize that *you* matter
- You're feeling less of a need to hide your true self
- You're starting to recognize how far you've come
- You're starting to believe in yourself

Healing doesn't happen all at once—it happens one small victory at a time.

Healing requires a lot of heavy lifting. It requires a commitment to show up for yourself day after day, even if it feels like you're falling apart. It requires you to do things that are uncomfortable and, at times, terrifying. It challenges you to face your fears and revisit feelings and memories you've tried so hard to leave behind. Healing may be some of the most difficult work of your lifetime (it certainly is for me). It's an internal journey, and while this work doesn't come with awards and accolades and milestones others can visibly see, you deserve to celebrate your progress every step of the way.

Give yourself credit for how far you've come: you've earned it.

CHAPTER 13

a setback
isn't a reset

In September 2018, I was feeling the best I had in over a year. I had made so much progress in the past six months that the nightmares that used to disrupt my sleep several nights a week had become rare. I learned and practiced coping skills and breathing exercises to ground myself, and anxiety that had seemed almost permanent only flared up occasionally. I learned how to manage and desensitize some of my triggers through exposure therapy, so they no longer led to panic each time I stumbled upon one. I hadn't had a panic attack in two months, and was feeling lighter and happier, and I was proud of how far I had come.

Then, on the morning of September 27, I cried for nearly four hours straight as I watched Christine Blasey Ford's testimony, when she bravely shared the story of the trauma she had experienced at a high school party when Supreme Court nominee Brett Kavanaugh sexually assaulted her. As I heard the chilling details of the assault and how she was able to escape, I was reminded of the traumas I'd experienced. I thought about the time I was assaulted by a man I'd been dancing with in Florida on spring break. I thought about the time a colleague trapped me at my desk as he kept trying to kiss me, and how I had to slide out from my chair and crawl under my desk to escape. I thought about what had happened to Andrea.

Later that afternoon, as I attempted to ground myself so I could get some work done, an Instagram notification popped up on my phone. As a social media consultant, my job involved managing social media on behalf of our clients, so when their accounts received a notification, I'd see them too. One of my clients had received a direct message from a bartender named Ryan. My heart dropped, and chills traveled through my body. It was him.

Usually, I'd ignore these notifications and let my employee read and respond to them, but I didn't want her to message him back and start a conversation with a sexual predator; I had to protect her. I tapped on the notification, shaking so hard that I could barely hold on to my phone. He wrote, "Hi there! I offer bartending services for weddings and private events in the Bay Area. If you ever need a bartender for an upcoming event, shoot me a message." *Oh my god*, I thought, *how is he still working?* I had blocked him on my personal social media accounts the morning after he assaulted Andrea, so I didn't have a clue where he was living or what he was doing for work. Last I heard, he was unemployed, since Joey fired him immediately after I had told him that Ryan drugged Andrea.

My heart raced as a million anxious thoughts ran through my mind. *He must know that my team is managing the social media. He knew I'd see his message. He must've picked today to send it because he's trying to mess with me. He wants me to know he's still out there, like Kavanaugh. He's going to find me and get revenge for getting him fired.*

I panicked, and I didn't know what to do, so I deleted the message and blocked him immediately. I thought that if I just got rid of him on social, then I could move on and get rid of him in real life.

For the rest of the day, I was on high alert. I peeked out my window constantly, scanning the streets and sidewalks to see if Ryan was lurking around in my neighborhood. I ran through my house, checking to make sure every door was locked and every window secure. I kept the key fob to our security system in my pocket, so I could press the panic button within seconds, if necessary.

That night, I had a nightmare. I couldn't remember exactly what it was about, but I knew Ryan was in it. I woke up in tears at 4:00 A.M., screaming, "HE'S A RAPIST!" and began panicking. For the next 30 minutes, I cried so hard that my eyes were swollen shut.

That day, I couldn't bring myself to leave the house; the outside world didn't feel safe because Ryan was somewhere out there. I had an appointment scheduled with a male doctor but canceled it because I was worried that he'd try to creep on me. And later that night, I didn't feel safe in my own home. I woke up in the middle of the night to go to the bathroom, and my heart was pounding. I had a strong feeling that someone was hiding in the shower, and I swore I saw a man's shadow behind the shower curtain. I quickly ran out of the bathroom, grabbed the key fob, and returned to the bathroom with my thumb hovering over the panic button. I took a deep breath, bracing myself for who I might find, and threw the shower curtain to one side to reveal who was there. Nobody was there; I was just seeing danger everywhere.

The weekend arrived, and as I spent time with friends, safety was reestablished, and I came back to reality. I realized that Ryan's message was an unlucky coincidence; he was just trying to sell his services to my client, and the timing couldn't have been worse. As I looked back at what had happened over the previous few days, I was disappointed with myself. I thought I was irresponsible for watching something that I knew would be triggering. I was unable to recognize my catastrophic thoughts and catch them before they spiraled out of control. I had another nightmare about Ryan, after working so hard to rewrite my dreams so that he no longer haunted me in my sleep. I had all the skills to manage my anxiety, yet it was once again so severe that I couldn't work for two days. I was a failure, and I felt like I was losing myself again.

In my next therapy session, I filled my therapist in on what had happened. I cried as I told her, "Just a few days before this happened, I was writing in my journal about how proud I was for all the progress I've made. And last week, I was basically back to where I was six months ago." I felt embarrassed, looking down to avoid eye contact.

"Reading that message must have been terrifying," she said gently. "It only makes sense that you'd experience PTSD symptoms again. There wasn't anything you could have done to prevent this from happening."

I soaked up my tears with a tissue, then looked up at her. "But I would have been able to handle it better if I didn't watch Dr. Ford's testimony that morning. I knew it was going to be triggering."

She shook her head. "It was important to you. Besides, her testimony was covered everywhere. Even if you wanted to avoid it, you wouldn't have been able to." She was right—I wouldn't have been able to go on any social media platform without seeing something about it. She paused for a moment and locked eyes with me to make sure I was hearing her, and then continued, "You have made a lot of progress—you still are. This doesn't mean you're regressing. You're learning from this, and you'll continue moving forward."

I was still upset with myself, so it was hard for me to take in what she was saying. But the next day, I felt calmer, and as I reflected on what my therapist had said, I realized that she was completely right. I noticed that even though I was triggered, I still had made progress. Sure, I couldn't work for two days because I was so shaken up, but before I started therapy, my anxiety was so bad that I wasn't able to work for two weeks. Before, I had nightmares four times a week, and that week I only had two nightmares. Before, I hid in my house and avoided seeing people for weeks if I had a panic attack, yet now I saw friends within days of getting triggered. I still experienced symptoms, but they were less frequent, and less intense. That's progress.

Setbacks don't erase the progress you've already made.

It was unrealistic to think that I'd never get triggered and experience PTSD symptoms again. Some triggers are completely unavoidable: we can't control everything that is going on in the world, and we can't control other people's actions. There was one time, at 7:30 in the morning, when my neighbor barged into my house after I repeatedly asked him to stay outside. I tried to keep the door shut, but he pushed his way in. I was panicking and yelling "Please go outside!" and he kept replying, "I'm your neighbor!" I thought (but couldn't say because I was hyperventilating), *I know you're my neighbor! But it doesn't matter! Get out of my house!* It was a very triggering experience, and there was literally nothing I could have done to avoid it.

And even if triggers are avoidable, we may not want to avoid them if that'll keep us from seeing people, going places, and doing things we love. For months, I passed up opportunities to see friends and go places because I was afraid that I would have a panic attack. I sent regrets to every invite I received to go to San Francisco because the city reminded me of my trauma, and as a result, I missed out on life. Since then, I've made an effort not to let my triggers keep me from the things I want.

No matter how much work we put into healing and how much progress we make, there will still be times when unexpected triggers hit us like a gut punch, and as a result, trauma symptoms flare-up. Your trauma symptoms may also resurface or intensify around the anniversary date of a traumatic experience, or a season in which it took place, as your mind and body has associated that time of year with danger and pain. The stress that comes along with life's challenges may also profoundly impact our mental health, making our trauma and symptoms feel even heavier.

When you're going through a rough patch, try not to be so hard on yourself. Setbacks don't erase all the progress that you've already made, and just because it feels like you've taken a few steps back, it doesn't mean you're back at square one. You can still suffer from nightmares, panic attacks, anxiety, and depression, *and* be healing. Healing may look like experiencing symptoms less frequently or for a shorter duration. Healing may look like having less intense symptoms. Healing may look like understanding your triggers better and noticing how you react to them. Healing is all about progress, and while setbacks feel discouraging, they can be a helpful part of our healing process, providing us with more information and an opportunity to grow.

Healing doesn't mean everything is fixed—it means you're learning to pick up the pieces, one piece at a time.

The next time your trauma symptoms start resurfacing, or if they become more intense, take some time to observe what's happening, and acknowledge your feelings, like we discussed in Chapter 3. Most often, panic attacks and other symptoms don't appear out of nowhere; sometimes, there's a trigger, and sometimes there are other factors involved that build up and lead to those symptoms. I've noticed that pretty much every panic attack I've had has taken place after a restless night of tossing and turning

in my sheets. Since I've made that connection, I've prioritized my sleep and developed a relaxing nighttime routine, which has been essential to my healing.

Start making your own connections by recalling
what you were doing the days prior to your symptoms
flaring up. Think back to see if any stressful situations at
work or school come to mind, or if you've had any challenges within your relationships. Think about if the date
or time of year has anything to do with one of your past
traumatic experiences. Think about how your sleep has
been, if your diet or appetite has changed at all, or if you
drank more caffeine or alcohol than usual. Think about
how your mood has been, and if there were any experiences that affected it. As you begin building a better
understanding of yourself and your symptoms, you can
use that information to uncover the areas you can work
on to continue progressing.

Open yourself up to the lessons the low points bring.

Healing isn't linear. This journey is filled with ups and downs, and when you hit a bump along the road, it might feel like you're back to where you started. But as you pick yourself back up and reflect on what happened, you'll likely find that you didn't travel backward at all. Obstacles may slow us down, but they don't transport us back to the beginning of our journeys. Setbacks are temporary, and they don't take away what you've accomplished so far. The valuable insights you gain during the low points will allow you to build on the progress you've already made, so that you can keep moving forward. And over time, you'll build resilience, so when you stumble upon a bumpy road, you'll have the experience to navigate it like a pro.

your story isn't over

Trauma can make it feel like you're a stranger to yourself. Going through something life-altering changes the way you view yourself and how you fit into the world. When trauma consumes your life, it might feel like your life is defined by your struggles and what you've been through. When it feels like your world has collapsed around you, you may lose sight of your purpose, and what matters. You may not know who you are and what you're doing with your life. You may not have a clue what brings you joy, and whether you even deserve it.

Since I'd experienced trauma at a young age, I spent most of my life feeling lost, but when I was 26, I thought I finally had all the answers. I knew the kind of person I wanted to be (kind, caring, smart, fun, passionate) and what I wanted to do with my life (social media consulting). I had a clear vision of what success looked like to me: a healthy and happy partnership with Adam, lots of friends, a growing business with Fortune 500 clients, a lovely home, and enough money to travel around the world. I did whatever I could to reach my goals and started on the right path. Then, two years later, around the time

I was diagnosed with PTSD, I felt like I'd completely lost myself again.

I used to be the fun friend who was always down for happy hour any night of the week, but I started declining every invite and stopped making plans with most people. I wanted a lot of friends, but found myself letting some friendships fall apart, partly because I was afraid to go places and partly because I didn't want them to see me struggling.

I used to be all about the hustle and would have done whatever it took to get more exposure, secure new clients, and grow my business. But with PTSD, I didn't have the energy to go above and beyond. There were many days when I could only do the bare minimum. When one client noticed and terminated my contract, I didn't even care; I actually felt a tiny sense of relief. I no longer felt passionate about the "dream job" I had worked so hard to create.

My hobbies no longer appealed to me. I used to blog and Instagram about food and drinks and write about social media and creativity but didn't feel inspired to create that type of content anymore. I loved photography and learning new camera tricks or editing skills, but I was no longer interested in pursuing any of that. I bought a new camera and ended up using it only twice.

At first, I thought this disconnection was coming from depression, since my psychiatrist had explained that losing interest in things is a common symptom. But even after the fog of depression had drifted away and I was able to think more clearly, I still felt lost. Even after I started to heal and felt ready to get my life together, I had no idea who I was and what I was passionate about anymore.

I became frustrated with myself. I felt stuck, like everyone around me was moving forward with their careers and personal lives, passing me by. I thought, *I had this all figured out. Why can't I go back to normal?* I'd get bitter and upset thinking about what my trauma had cost me. I lost time and energy trying to get my symptoms under control. I lost clients and money. I lost friends and missed out on events and trips and other fun activities because I was too anxious to leave the house. I lost my vision and purpose. I lost myself.

As I got further into my healing journey, I started to see things from a different perspective. I began recognizing the ways in which my healing had helped me become a better version of myself. I used to ignore my feelings and my needs, and through healing, I became more emotionally intelligent, which helped me in every aspect of my life. Struggling taught me how to ask for help, and challenged me to be vulnerable with others, which strengthened some of my relationships. Learning to hold space for my pain helped me become more skilled at holding space for others' pain. Healing taught me how to address my problems head-on rather than avoiding them. I became more compassionate and supportive toward survivors and others going through hardships, which made me want to be more generous and advocate for others.

When I looked back to reexamine my losses, I realized that they weren't really losses. The friendships that fell apart created space for me to build deeper relationships with those I value most. I thought I'd lost time healing, but in reality, it helped advance my personal development. While I'll never be thankful for having experienced trauma or grateful for all the pain and suffering I've been through, healing helped me become a person I'm proud of.

Healing isn't about repairing yourself—it's about becoming yourself.

When my world shattered after trauma, I tried my best to sweep up the pieces and restore what my life was before. I battled myself as I tried to accomplish the impossible task of fixing something that wasn't fixable. It wasn't possible to go back in time and undo what I'd gone through. My view of the world changed. *I* changed. My life would never be the same as it used to be. And since I had started to recognize my growth, I didn't see that as such a bad thing.

Losing sight of who I had been pushed me to reflect on my values and reevaluate my priorities. I found myself asking questions like, *What matters most to me at this point of my life? What does success look like to me now?* After turning inward, I discovered that who I was no longer aligned with who I wanted to be. Before, mental health wasn't even on my radar, whereas now I discovered that self-care is my number one priority, as I learned that it's challenging to find joy and be there for others when I'm not in a good place mentally and emotionally. I discovered that money no longer motivated me, and that making an excessive amount of it was no longer part of my definition of success. I discovered that I needed work to be low stress so that I could create space for my healing, and started maintaining a lighter workload, setting boundaries with clients, and taking the weekends off. I discovered that hustle culture no longer served me and that I wanted to invest more time in nurturing relationships that did. I discovered that I didn't want a lot of not-so-close friends to drink with; I wanted to connect deeper and have intimate friendships with a couple of people I could be vulnerable with. I discovered that I still wanted to write and create on social media, but I wanted to create content to support other trauma survivors like me. Instead of an exciting life jet-setting around the world, I discovered that I wanted a slow and peaceful life with people who help me feel safe.

Before, I felt like I was moving through life, doing what I thought I should be doing based on society's definition of success (money and power). I lost my identity to trauma, but that loss turned out to be a gift: it gave me the opportunity to ask myself what I really wanted out of life and allowed me to create a new blueprint for how I wanted to spend my time. While there were still plenty of painful phases where I felt like I was barely getting by, overall, life became so much more fulfilling than I ever imagined it could be.

Just because you've had a hard life doesn't mean you can't have a fulfilling life.

I don't know what your life was like before, and I don't know how trauma changed things for you. I was in a privileged position to begin with, and with a supportive partner by my side, I didn't end up losing much. You may have lost a whole lot more than I have. You may require more time to grieve a relationship or career that ended, the future you had planned, or the loss of a community or someone you loved. Your losses may cause so much more added stress and make each day that much harder to get through. Your losses may have left you with a hollowness in your soul that might seem impossible to fill. If you're going through this, I'm so sorry.

I don't have all the answers, but I do know that, like trauma, grief needs to be processed—not pushed away—and it may feel less heavy as you work through it over time. Grieving is part of healing, so take all the time you need. There's no need to force a positive perspective or find the silver lining if that isn't where you are on your journey. Healing isn't about transforming your negatives into positives or minimizing your pain; it's about holding space for your pain and learning to hold space for goodness too.

I also know that you, a trauma survivor, have an inner strength that's already within you, whether you realize it's there or not. Things may not be okay right now, and everything might feel like it's falling apart—but *you* will be okay, and I know you have it in you to make it through this.

I wish there were a rewind button on life, but unfortunately, this isn't our reality. It isn't possible to return to the lives we had before trauma, and I found that wishing I could go back in time only caused more pain and frustration, creating a storm within myself that made it impossible to keep moving forward. Our only choice is to try the best we can to create better futures for ourselves.

Just because your life won't be the same doesn't mean that it's completely ruined; your story isn't over yet. It's possible to live a fulfilling life after trauma. It's possible to find happiness and love and whatever else you desire after trauma, and you don't have to minimize or mask your pain to do so. You can carry your pain *and* build a meaningful life. You can carry your grief *and* grow into a person that you're proud of. These things can coexist; they aren't mutually exclusive. Trauma wasn't your choice, and you didn't sign up for the challenges you've faced as a result. But you can choose to rebuild, reorienting your life toward more fulfilling goals, which can make it easier to find the joy you deserve.

Trauma isn't the end of the world—it's the beginning of something new.

Redefining Your Values

While it may take some time and healing to notice, trauma provides us with different perspectives, bringing new meaning to our lives. After life-changing experiences, our priorities often change with us. Things you thought were once incredibly important, like, for example, material things, may not hold the same value after your world has turned upside down. The struggles we face often highlight what we've taken for granted in the past, whether that's our health, resources, loved ones, safety, or life itself.

It's important to redefine your values as you're healing so you know how you want to rebuild and the direction you want to grow. Our values help us determine what makes up a meaningful life, and as you realign yourself toward something that feels true to the person you're becoming, and not who you used to be, the happier you'll become. If your values aren't clear to you now, that's okay. Healing isn't about knowing all the answers and having everything figured out; it's about lingering in the questions for as long as you need to until the answers present themselves. Our values change as we heal too—nothing about healing is fixed.

Determine What Matters Most

Ask yourself, *What matters most to me now?* Think about the things that are important to you and what you're passionate about. If it helps, think about times when you feel your best and most fulfilled, and the times you feel the most like yourself. Maybe what matters most to you is health, your family, love, and faith—or maybe it's community, creativity, education, and generosity. As long as it feels true to you, there are no wrong answers. If you have a long list, narrow it down to the top five; there's only so much you can do, so it's important to prioritize.

Also, take note of what *isn't* as important to you now. Maybe your career was your number one priority before, and now you realize that your mental health is more important than climbing the corporate ladder. Maybe there's a hobby or relationship that no longer serves you.

Determining what isn't as important may help make what *is* important more clear.

Align Your Life with Your Values

What adjustments can you make to create more space for what matters most? Think about the things you could do to create more time for your priorities, and if it's possible, spend less of your time and energy on things that no longer hold the same value. If you find that you value your relationships more now, make an effort to deepen them. If you value your community, think about ways in which you can engage with it or give back. If you have a stressful job with a demanding boss that makes you feel burnt-out, it may be time to start searching for a new opportunity where you'll have more time to recharge. It can be scary and overwhelming to completely change directions in life, like embarking on a new career path that's completely different from what you've done before—but if that's what's calling you, great! So I suggest starting slow. You don't have to go through monumental changes and a massive transformation to create a more fulfilling life; small changes within our existing lives may be just as meaningful.

You won't want to go 'back to normal' once you see the gifts healing offers.

99

Trauma reroutes our lives. It leads us down paths we never expected or wanted, and it can be absolutely devastating to lose yourself and a life you cherished. And yet, as you develop a better understanding of who you are now, you may find that your old way of living no longer serves you. While some of the change trauma brings will negatively impact your life, the growth you experience through healing can positively impact your life.

Growth often emerges out of struggle. When things are effortless, we don't have to dig deep and push ourselves the way we do when life tests us. Most of my personal growth has come out of the most strenuous and painful times of my life. Living in fear can force the courage inside of you to surface. Feeling overwhelmed often pushes you to ask for support, forming deeper and nurturing relationships. Not giving up when you desperately want to often reveals the inner strength and resilience you never knew existed. Struggling with your mental health can lead you to become more empathetic and compassionate toward others who are struggling. Even though trauma leads to pain and destruction, there are benefits to be found on this journey as well.

While you cannot restore what your life was before trauma, you have the opportunity to create a new path back to yourself—and you may find it's led you to a more joyful way of living.

CHAPTER 15

staying silent benefits no one

There's so much stigma attached to mental health struggles. While I didn't realize it at the time, it's the main reason I kept my traumatic experiences and PTSD diagnosis a secret for months. As someone living with a mental illness, I didn't want to be seen as weak or crazy, unstable or dangerous. Whenever something tragic happens, like gun violence, people often place the blame on mental illness, saying things like "mental illness pulls the trigger, not the gun," and it stigmatizes these conditions further. And when the media highlighted people with PTSD as aggressive and violent, I didn't want to be associated with such actions. As I discussed in Chapter 8, I was ashamed of my condition, and that shame damaged my self-esteem.

Internalizing public stigma makes it more challenging to heal, and it also prevents many of us from reaching out for support in the first place. Even if someone knows something isn't right and wants to get better, they may believe that they'll be judged for their mental health struggles. They may be worried about potential discrimination by people around them. So they may try to "be strong" and ignore the symptoms and keep what they're going through to themselves. And as you've learned from my experience, ignoring feelings doesn't work, and keeping struggles a secret will prevent a person from building the support system they need to heal.

There's a lot of misinformation about trauma and mental health conditions out there, and it's to everyone's benefit to shatter these stereotypes and create a world where we don't need to hide ourselves, and don't have to be ashamed for what we've been through. Remember, your healing always comes first, and none of this is required. But once you feel ready, if you want to help fight the stigma and advocate for others like us, consider sharing your story.

Your Voice Matters

For the longest time, I kept my story locked away because I believed that struggling with trauma and my mental health was shameful. Shame wanted me to make myself as small as possible, stay quiet, and hide what I'd been going through. But once I started healing, I realized that my story didn't end with trauma and pain; it also included the healing and growth that followed. I slowly began sharing my journey with others, and as I practiced being vulnerable with those who helped me feel safe, the shame started to melt away.

When I think about some of the most healing experiences for me, the moments that come to mind are those where I've given voice to the parts of me that were trapped in the shadow of shame. It allowed me to connect deeper with people, and when others reciprocated and shared their stories with me, I realized that I wasn't the only one in the world on this journey. It was empowering, for myself and others. Keeping our trauma and healing a secret only validates the idea that we should be ashamed of what we've gone through. But when we bring our stories to light, we send a powerful message that trauma is part of life for so many of us, and it lets others who are suffering in silence know that they are not alone.

In Chapter 9, we discussed opening up to your friends and family and those closest to you for support on your healing journey. When it comes to fighting stigma and advocating for others, your support system is a great place to start. Aside from telling them about your trauma (however much you decide to share) and leaning on them when you're going through a rough patch, try to talk to them about mental health and healing even when you're feeling your best. Remember, healing isn't just about pain and struggle: it's about the growth and goodness too.

Before I began having these conversations more regularly, my anxiety would flare up whenever I thought about talking to someone about trauma and healing, whether the conversation was about me or not. Without practice, these conversations made me uncomfortable, which made them difficult (and sometimes impossible) to have. I've learned that talking about healing when I'm *not* struggling makes discussions that take place when I *am* struggling easier, both for me and those in my support system. You could start sharing your wins along your healing journey (and celebrate with them!). You could send them an article or social media post about mental health, trauma, or healing that resonates with you. You could tell them about something that you learned in therapy. Again, it's completely up to you to choose who you open up to and how much you share, so do whatever feels right for you. Just remember that the more we talk about trauma and healing, the more comfortable everyone feels having these conversations.

And the more comfortable people are having them, the better position we're in to support one another.

I've made it a point to work mental health and healing into everyday conversations. I've brought up how cardio helps with my anxiety as I was chatting with a woman on a bike next to me while we waited for our spin class to start. I'd tell my employee and clients when I'd have therapy and wouldn't be available, instead of making up an excuse. I'd share what my therapist has told me with my friends (and sometimes, everyone on social media). Of course, you don't need to be as open as I am, and it may not be safe for you to be. But if you are able to, try to normalize these conversations around mental health, even if it's only with those closest to you, because every time we have them, the stigma deteriorates.

If you've become more comfortable sharing with your support system, consider expanding the inner circle to include others. The more people hear your story about healing from trauma, the more people will have a better understanding of trauma and how it affects people. If you only told your best friend about what you're going through, think about sharing with other friends who you may not be as close to, but are still comfortable with. If those conversations go well, think of others who you might want to share with. It may be anxiety-provoking when you start, given how vulnerability is a practice, but the more you have these conversations, the easier they'll become.

Your story could be the road map for someone else's healing journey.

Once I got to the point in my healing where I recognized my growth, I became overwhelmed with a desire to share my story on social media so other survivors like me wouldn't feel so alone. It was incredibly freeing and empowering, and to my surprise, it also opened other avenues of support with people already in my network. Sharing with an audience outside of my inner circle helped me identify people who want to have conversations about healing and other things that matter, online and offline. It was one of the best things that I've done for my healing.

I know broadcasting personal news to the world isn't everyone's style, but if you do have a desire to share on social media publicly, an important tip: make sure those who are closest to you know in advance. I say this for two reasons: 1) Some people are on social media more than others, and due to the algorithms, people who follow you aren't guaranteed to see the content you post—which means that if you're hoping to fill in the people you're close to this way, it's possible that they won't even see your posts. 2) Social media isn't a good way to find out about important news from people close to you: it's impersonal.

175

So I recommend sharing with people you really care about *before* you share it on social media. This will make them feel like they're important to you and will likely increase the chances that they'll be willing to provide support when you need it.

Sharing your story openly creates a domino effect with a lasting impact; it inspires others to share their stories and heal as well. When Christine Blasey Ford testified in front of the Senate Judiciary Committee, the Rape, Abuse & Incest National Network (RAINN) announced that the number of calls to its National Sexual Assault Hotline jumped by 201 percent that day (Yan 2018). Dr. Ford's testimony showed sexual assault survivors that they aren't alone, which motivated so many others to speak out. Clearly, the testimony was televised and reached millions of people, but you can still have an impact on a much smaller scale.

Shortly after I began sharing about my healing journey on social media, a friend told me she was inspired and decided to blog about her experience with abuse. A colleague of mine told me she was "following my lead" by opening up about her addiction and journey to sobriety. And later, when I started @HealingFromPTSD on Instagram, each week, several survivors would tag me in their powerful posts about how they're healing from trauma, and I'm sure they've inspired others as well.

Using your voice can be incredibly healing, not just for you, but for so many others within your community. When we share our stories of trauma and healing, it often validates someone else's experience and helps them release their shame. Healing can feel so isolating, and just knowing that we aren't on this journey alone is incredibly powerful. Your story of healing may inspire other survivors to embark on their own healing journeys and give them the hope to keep going. Your story doesn't have to be perfect and complete; it can be messy and a work-in-progress, just as you are, and it may even resonate more with people that way. When you show others your full humanity, it gives them permission to be fully human too. Give people a glimpse of the mountains you're climbing and the twists and turns along the way, and you'll leave them thinking, *If they can get through this, I can too.*

Let's Put an End to Victim-Blaming

Aside from the stigma, another thing that significantly contributes to the shame surrounding trauma is victim-blaming. So many of us haven't shared our stories because we fear people will blame us—and that fear is completely valid. While victim-blaming is closely associated with traumatic experiences like sexual assault and intimate partner violence, most trauma survivors have been blamed for their trauma, regardless of the type of traumatic experience.

When people hear about something traumatic happening to someone, their first instinct is often to question the victim and point out what they could have done differently. *They shouldn't have been there. They should have left earlier. They drank too much.* Or they question the victim's actions (or lack of action). *Why didn't they speak up sooner? What were they wearing?* I experienced this myself. In college, a roommate asked me, "Why did you even dance with him?" after I told her that a stranger at a club had sexually assaulted me. According to some friends, I should have walked to the police station when I first noticed the man following me, and I should have watched Ryan pour the drinks. In their eyes, I could have prevented the traumas from happening, and it was my fault for failing to do so. They didn't realize it, but they were victim-blaming.

Many of us grew up with this belief that good things happen to good people, and bad things happen to bad people; the world is fair and we're in control of what happens to us. This messaging was drilled into us by parents and other authority figures who wanted kids to behave; we were rewarded with cookies when we were "good" and were put on time-out (or worse) when we were "bad." So we've grown into adults who believe that if we're ethical, work hard, and stay out of trouble, bad things won't happen to us. Therefore, many people feel a need when something awful happens to someone to justify why that experience has happened to them and identify where they went wrong.

This belief also explains why we blame ourselves for the traumas we experience; we believe we could have done something better, or done more, so it must have been our fault. But as we discussed in Chapter 6, terrible things can happen to anyone at any time, and the victim is never to blame. But so many people, especially those who haven't gone through their own traumatic experiences, may not understand this.

I believe every survivor should have the opportunity to share their story without fear of being judged or blamed; it would provide healing for them and so many others. So in order to make it easier for survivors to come forward and bring their stories to light, we must put an end to victim-blaming.

Together, we can make the world feel safer for trauma survivors.

My therapist prepped me for standing up to victim-blamers when she pulled me out of my cycle of self-blame and helped me realize that Ryan was the only person responsible for Andrea's assault. Before that session, I struggled to speak up. Whenever I heard someone victim-blaming, even though they weren't talking about me, I felt like I was under attack. With my heart racing, I'd think, *If they believe that so-and-so is to blame for their trauma, they must believe that I am to blame for mine.* I still get anxious whenever I have a conversation with someone who is victim-blaming. Sometimes, I'm livid and don't even want to engage because it feels like I'll explode. But the world would feel a whole lot safer for trauma survivors if victim-blaming was put to an end, so at the very least, when I hear someone victim-blaming, I try to question their views like my therapist questioned mine.

Over lunch one day, someone had told me about how one of her "friends" was sexually assaulted at a party by a co-worker. I told her, "That's awful."

She agreed, "It is." She started stabbing at her spinach salad, then added, "But she shouldn't have been drinking so much."

My heart dropped. I was shocked to hear that coming from her. Anxiety rose up inside me as I attempted to tell her something similar to what my therapist told me. "But that doesn't matter. Her drinking didn't cause him to assault her."

She shrugged and said, "Yeah, I know."

I took her acknowledgment as a signal that the conversation was coming to an end, and I started playing with the soggy paper straw in my water glass. But then I heard her say, "I just don't get why she hasn't left the company yet."

I looked up at her. Heart racing, I asked, "Why is she the one who should leave? She didn't do anything wrong. If someone should leave, it's him."

She nodded and said, "That's fair."

We sat in silence for a few seconds. She must've picked up on how irritated I was, as she went on to say, "Sorry, I just didn't think about it that way."

People slip into the cycle of victim-blaming without realizing it, and if they're going to change, they need to be aware that they're doing it in the first place. People don't think they're victim-blamers, so if you explicitly tell them to "stop victim-blaming," they may get defensive and disagree with whatever you're saying because they've been criticized. Instead, we should provide them with an alternative perspective so they come to their own realization that their thinking patterns might be limited. You don't need to get into details and have a full-on debate. If you hear someone commenting on what a victim was wearing, where they were, how much they were drinking, or how late they were out, even a response as simple as "That doesn't matter. It's not their fault," or "The only person to blame is the perpetrator," will help enforce the fact that it wasn't, and never is, the victim's fault.

I know how difficult this can be, especially if you're a person who tends to avoid confrontation. You may find it easier to stand up for others than to stand up for yourself. When you're not the one directly under attack, it might feel less risky to speak up. But if the topic of discussion reminds you of your trauma, and you believe participating in the conversation could potentially trigger anxiety or panic, it may make sense not to engage. See how you feel in each situation, and don't force yourself to take a stand if it feels overwhelming.

One of the most healing experiences can be helping someone else realize they aren't alone.

Most of us know how painful it is to be invalidated, dismissed, and not believed. We know how damaging it is to be blamed for our trauma, and how isolating it is when the world sends a message that we ought to be ashamed for struggling. Sometimes what happens after a traumatic experience requires just as much healing as the event itself, and it shouldn't have to be that way. I believe each one of us has a powerful story to tell, and our voices could be a force for change.

I have this strong desire to help others, but it isn't because I'm a selfless person: I'm no saint. It's because I noticed that when I advocate for others and for what I believe in, it makes me feel better; using my voice has helped me heal.

Trauma left me feeling powerless, and sharing my story was one way that I reclaimed my power. When people better understand me, I feel safer being around them as I don't have to hide parts of myself. Speaking up and shutting down victim-blamers makes me feel empowered. Listening and "being there" for other trauma survivors struggling with difficult times helps me feel connected and closer to my community. Helping people feel less alone has made *me* feel less alone. Giving is a gift in itself, and if you're in a position to help others, it might help you heal too.

As good as it can feel to support others and stand up for what you believe in, remember to prioritize your mental health. If you're already feeling anxious, being vulnerable with someone you're not super comfortable with could lead you to feel even more anxious. If you think engaging with someone who just made a snarky comment about a victim in a high-profile case might lead to panic, it probably makes the most sense to walk away. Standing up to someone isn't worth a panic attack, so it's more than okay if you can't bring yourself to speak up just yet.

There will be a day when your symptoms soften, your gratitude will overflow, and you'll want to pay it forward, but until then, take care of yourself.

CHAPTER 16

embrace the ongoing process

In November 2019, I thought my healing journey was coming to an end. After nearly two years of trauma therapy and prioritizing my healing, I thought my work was complete. I hadn't had a panic attack in eight months and couldn't remember the last time I had a nightmare or flashback. I was able to quell my anxiety when it surfaced, so such occurrences were brief. I was moving through the world with less fear and had reconnected with joy. I was able to revisit my traumatic experiences without tears streaming from my eyes, losing my breath, or feeling unsafe. I was openly sharing my story about how I'd triumphed over trauma and believed I'd reached the peak of the mountain I'd been climbing. I thought I was *healed* and didn't think there was any more work to be done.

I have never been more wrong.

Like everyone else in the world, I faced many challenges in 2020. I said good-bye to my *ông ngoại* and attended my first Facebook Live funeral. As businesses closed, I lost clients, and my stress went through the roof as I tried to figure out how I could keep paying my employee's salary. As hate crimes against Asian Americans multiplied, I feared for my family's safety as I saw stories of people who looked like my mom, aunties, and uncles getting brutally attacked. I started @HealingFromPTSD on Instagram, and aside from the cold criticism and mean-spirited comments I faced on some of my posts, I received threats and went through periods of nonstop harassment as I started talking more about racial trauma, causing my anxiety to worsen to the greatest degree since my PTSD diagnosis. I received an anonymous e-mail from someone who claimed they went to school with me that said it was ironic that I am helping people in the way I am now since I was so terrible when I was younger. It triggered flashbacks from my child-hood, when I was harming myself and desperately wanted to end my life. I was depressed.

The trauma manifested physically too. There was a sharp, excruciating pain in my stomach that made it impos-sible to sleep, work, or eat anything other than plain toast for a week. The diagnosis was stomach ulcers, and after a series of lab tests, the cause was unknown. My doctor asked, "Have you been under a lot of stress?" It was the only explanation. The ulcers would clear up with meds, and then return, the cycle repeating itself for six months. With constant pain physically, emotionally, and mentally, 2020 was one of the hardest years of my adult life.

While I felt like I have fully healed from the two major events in my adulthood that led to my PTSD, 2020 revealed so many parts of me that still needed healing. I needed to heal from the loss of a grandfather, and the guilt I felt for not ever being able to have a real conversation with him. As conversations around racial justice spiked following the murders of George Floyd, Breonna Taylor, Ahmaud Arbery, and so many other Black and brown folks, it brought attention to wounds caused by racism and xenophobia within my family, and within our society, that I'd always invalidated due to my privilege. I had to dig into why I was so anxious when people criticized and insulted me online, which revealed existing wounds from my childhood of never feeling like I was enough. I had to address the pain I felt as a child and the harm I had inflicted on myself—something I'd previously detached myself from and left in the past. I had to learn how to show my younger, traumatized self compassion for the things she'd done to cope that I'd never consider doing now. I had to learn not to leave my younger self behind and reconcile who I once was with who I am now. My work was far from over, and it still is.

Healing has many layers; once you peel one back, another opportunity to heal often reveals itself.

You may think that there are experiences that don't require healing, and then something unexpected happens that leads you to reexamine those experiences again. I thought that I was "over" my self-harm from half a lifetime ago, and that it didn't have anything to do with what I was going through, but the depression triggered by those memories told me otherwise. I also thought that I was "over" being sexually assaulted in college, because I wasn't raped, so I didn't think it was a big deal. However, feeling dread in my stomach every time my partner touched me in a similar way was an indication that I had some healing to do.

You may think that you've completely healed from a traumatic experience, and then something happens that uncovers new triggers and a new piece of your trauma that you'd never thought about before. Sometimes, our traumatic experiences completely disappear from our memories, and then they come back when we get triggered, just like the experience I shared in Chapter 2 about my childhood trauma resurfacing decades later. Remember, our brains want to protect us, and as a result, we may experience memory loss. But when something triggers a traumatic memory, it can all come back along with a cascade of emotions, and healing may require us to sort through it.

Healing from trauma isn't just about working through the bigger traumatic events that happened; it's also about untangling the deep-seated beliefs that we're unworthy, unlovable, insignificant, or not enough, and addressing the events that instilled these beliefs. Sometimes, we don't even notice we hold such beliefs since they've slowly developed over several years (or perhaps our entire lifetimes), and it feels like they're part of who we are. It took a long time for these beliefs to form, and it can take just as long to unlearn them. It may be hard to let go because it's all we know, and the unknown can be terrifying. For many of us, unlearning inaccurate beliefs may be a lifelong practice.

At some point on your healing journey, you may be confronted with new hardships that cause the wounds you thought you'd healed from to start aching again, or create fresh wounds that hadn't previously existed. As we dis-cussed in Chapter 6, horrible things like trauma, illness, and loss are all part of life's challenges, and most often, we can't prevent them. It's unrealistic to think that we can escape all suffering. Facing these challenges is never easy, and experiencing them doesn't get easier; they may hit just as hard, and if they disturb areas where we're already hurting, the pain can compound, making it even harder to sit with. But as you continue healing, you'll be in a bet-ter position to face them, and better equipped to get back on your feet. You won't be starting at square one: you'll have the wisdom you've gained from earlier in your jour-ney to help you through it. You'll know what activities are healing for you. You'll have more self-awareness and a better understanding of your needs. You'll know how to process your feelings and practice self-compassion. You'll know which people you can count on for support. All of the healing work you're doing now is preparing you to take on any other challenges that life throws your way. The effort you put into healing will never go to waste; it makes you more resilient each day.

Your trauma didn't make you stronger—how you handled it did.

99

2020 was one of the most challenging years, but it was also one of my most transformative years. Since I'd already done so much healing work, I was in the best position I could have possibly been in to handle it. It wasn't easy, and I still have a long way to go, but little by little, I started feeling more at ease, more peaceful, and more *me*. As I turned inward, I discovered parts of myself that I'd suppressed and started to hold space for them. As I reflected on past experiences, I saw how they shaped me, which allowed me to start letting go of the beliefs that no longer served me. I felt like I was slowly growing into the person I was meant to be, which brought so much relief. Trekking through rough terrain led me to shed layers and allowed me to evolve into a more authentic version of myself.

I used to wish that my healing journey would just be over already. I just wanted to be done with the work and the pain so I could move on with my life. But now, I realize that being fully "healed" is a myth: it's impossible to avoid everything in life that causes pain. Whether an experience from your distant past bleeds into the present, or something new comes up, there will always be something we need to heal from.

I also realize that if my experiences hadn't pushed me toward self-reflection, I would have missed out on getting to know parts of myself that I never knew existed. While healing might be messy, inconvenient, exhausting, and distressing, new paths appear that allow you to explore yourself deeper when a new opportunity to heal arises. So much self-discovery and understanding unfolds throughout the process that can change your life and lead to joy, happiness, and inner peace. There's so much more to healing than the parts that hurt; it can just take some time (and work) for them to surface.

You can't be behind on your own healing journey. Take your time.

Healing is a long journey that goes on for miles, so be sure to pace yourself. If you've experienced multiple traumatic experiences, you may need to take it one trauma at a time, as trying to work through too much at once can be overwhelming. We can also get burnt out if we don't give ourselves a break from the deep healing work that drains our emotional resources. Sometimes, you may need breaks so you can get through a particularly stressful time at work or school, or if it's feeling like too much and you need to step away. Healing work doesn't always have to be intense reflections and turning inward. It isn't sustainable to keep digging, to keep trying to understand ourselves, and to keep processing nonstop, and it can be counterproductive to keep trying to force healing and "aha" moments. Walking away from exploration for a little might provide you with a new perspective that creates richer areas to delve into when you come back. Sometimes healing looks like disconnecting for a little bit and creating more space to bond with others, to find joy, rest, and laugh. Sometimes it looks like letting go and allowing yourself to fully live in the moment. Sometimes, healing is practicing being present instead of digging into the past.

Before, I thought my healing would pause when I'd take a break from the intense healing work. I'd think, *There's so much more to understand. I still have a long way to go; I don't have time to waste.* But taking a mini vacation is not wasted time. I noticed that when I check out for a bit, whether for a week or two, or a month or two, I feel lighter, and I often come back ready to explore deeper. And unlike a vacation from work, I'm able to ease back into it in my own time. It's okay to let yourself rest—your healing isn't going anywhere. Just remember that there's a difference between resting and avoiding: resting *supports* our healing by allowing us to refuel, whereas avoidance typically comes from a place of fear, and will continue fueling our fears, making it harder to heal.

Embrace the detours and reroutes along the way.

Healing is an ongoing, continuous process that ebbs and flows. There will be peaks and valleys and rivers to cross. There will be unanticipated reroutes and detours brought on by the inevitable challenges of life. While the harder, more painful moments may be tougher to get through, they can guide you to unexpected, mysterious paths that lead you toward beautiful moments. Beautiful moments of connection. Beautiful moments of self-discovery and understanding. Beautiful moments of compassion, wonder, and generosity. Beautiful moments of growth. Healing is a lifelong process, and as it pushes us to explore, try new things, and get creative with our lives, so much goodness is there to be found along the way.

We may never be fully "healed," but I don't see it as a bad thing. Healing is an art, and we're all masterpieces in the making.

conclusion

Healing is an incredible journey. I spent most of my life believing that I was damaged beyond repair and had no idea that trauma had anything to do with it. I was ashamed and brushed the experiences that had shook me to the side and ended up suffering in isolation. When I was diagnosed with PTSD, I thought that it was the end of the world, and I didn't believe I'd ever live a "normal" life after trauma, let alone grow into a person I could be proud of. As someone who spent years trying to run away from their traumatic experiences, desperately trying to forget all about them, I never thought I'd be here, writing a book and sharing my story with the world.

When I first embarked on this journey, I was let down. I thought healing was supposed to be filled with warm, feel-good moments and groundbreaking epiphanies—a comforting and inspiring process that would extract my pain. I thought that healing would be a "before and after" situation that happened all at once, where I'd go through an overnight transformation and then move on with my life. I thought my work would be complete once I was completely symptom-free. I had this vision of what I thought my healing journey should look like, and thought I was failing when it wasn't anything like I'd pictured.

Now that I've been on this journey for four years and have worked through the grief, the pain, and the parts that felt impossible to get through, I can tell you that it turned out to be so much more rewarding than I had ever imagined it being.

Before, I wanted someone to fix me—to wave a magic wand and send me back in time to when things were "normal," before my trauma symptoms swallowed me whole. Little did I know that I had a false sense of normalcy. "Normal" to me was ignoring my thoughts, pushing my feelings away, and suppressing parts of myself that I thought I should be ashamed of. "Normal" was dismissing and invalidating my experiences, and feeling like I wasn't enough. "Normal" was doing what I thought I should be doing based on other people's expectations without considering what I really wanted. Even if I could go back in time and undo the damage my trauma has caused, if it meant losing the insights and wisdom I've gained through healing, I wouldn't be interested in it at all.

It may take you some time to get here. You may have gone through more intense, destructive, traumatic experiences that will be more complicated to work through. You may be facing daily challenges that I have never had to face, adding to your stress. I know not everyone is as fortunate as I am, and I wish it didn't have to be that way. I wish everyone was paid a living wage and had access to housing, clean water, and food. I wish health care was free. Trauma isn't a choice, and everyone should have access to the same resources regardless of their employment and socioeconomic background. While these privileges don't erase the pain, they absolutely make it more manageable to navigate through.

Living in an environment where you feel unsafe makes healing more challenging. I have been a target of sexual assault and harassment, and there have been times when I haven't been able to walk down the street without being catcalled, which makes my heart race every time. But having light skin and being able to pass as a white person provides security that people with dark skin and non-European features don't have. For many people of color, queer people, and disabled folks, safety is a luxury. Whenever there is a violent story of a hate crime in the news, it impacts every person in that community, adding to the pain, stress, and fear already carried. While so much of healing comes from within, the environments you live in play a role as well. Not everything is in your control on this journey, so remember to be patient with yourself throughout the process. Take it one step at a time, one day at a time, and allow yourself to heal at your own speed.

Your journey may have more obstacles than mine, but that doesn't mean healing is out of reach. Healing is an internal process, and while external factors can help you along the way, the hidden power that lies within you is what fuels your journey. Healing is possible for *everyone*, and I hope this book has empowered you to begin charting your own path. I said it before, and I'll say it again: healing isn't a passive activity. Time won't magically heal your wounds and make everything better, so it's up to you to put the work in. You don't need to make drastic life changes or be in the "perfect" environment to start your healing journey—you can start now, and sometimes the simplest activities and minor adjustments can make a huge difference.

There are so many paths you can take on this journey, and finding the activities and practices that are most helpful to you takes some trial and error. If the road you're currently on isn't serving you, you have the power to change the course. There is always another way, another option, and you're allowed to change your mind at any point. Reroutes and U-turns aren't a waste of time—every bit of information you gain about yourself and your experiences will help prepare you for the next part of your journey.

When you're going through a rough patch, remember to meet yourself with compassion. When we criticize and shame ourselves, we sometimes get so stuck on what went wrong, or what we wish we could have done differently, that it keeps us from moving forward. Let yourself be fully human. Let yourself feel however you feel and learn from your mistakes. Remember that healing is a messy journey, and setbacks are often part of the process, so don't be hard on yourself when such a thing happens. Once you make it through, you may realize that you were healing all along.

Healing is a long journey, and it can take some time to find the people who help you along the way. Remember that if anyone makes you feel like you're less than or "damaged" or not enough, you deserve better. If someone constantly invalidates your trauma and dismisses your feelings, you deserve better. If someone doesn't respect your boundaries, you deserve better. Not everyone will be able to provide the support you deserve on your healing journey, and just because a few people can't be there for you doesn't mean you won't find someone who will.

Every couple of months, take a moment to slow down and reflect on your journey. Life is busy, and when you're juggling work or school with your social life and everything that goes into healing, it may be impossible to notice your progress. Recognizing the improvements you're making, no matter how small they might seem, will continue to fuel your journey. Give yourself credit for your progression and let yourself celebrate these small wins. You deserve it.

Sharing my story has played a critical role in my healing journey, and one day in the future, I hope you're inspired to share yours. You might think that your story doesn't matter, that it isn't different or traumatic enough, or that people in your life won't care or can't relate. But your story is important, and it does matter. It could even be the healing guide someone else in your life needs. If nothing else, opening up to others about your experiences will help you release the pain and shame attached to your trauma, and make you feel lighter. There's no rush, but once you feel ready, start sharing.

If you're having a really hard time right now, I'm so sorry. I know how painful things can be, and I know what it's like to want to give up. Sometimes when you're healing, things feel like they're getting worse before they start getting better. This is natural; healing isn't linear. There will be highs and lows, and even if you're making progress, healing doesn't always feel good. At times, it may be overwhelming, confusing, incredibly lonely, and excruciatingly painful. If you feel like it's too much to handle, and don't know how to navigate through your pain, reach out for help. We all need a little extra help sometimes. Having enough self-awareness to recognize your limitations is a strength; don't let the fear of being "weak" keep you from getting the support you deserve.

Even with the pain and devastation, there's so much joy and goodness that can be found on this journey too. Your story is far from over, and it's possible to live a fulfilling life after trauma, even if the pain doesn't completely disappear. Healing may be some of the most challenging work you do in life, but the good news is, I've found that the most difficult work often ends up being the most rewarding.

No matter how hard things get, don't give up on the person you're becoming. There will be a day when the heaviness melts away, and you'll look back on the miles you've traveled with pride and think, *I made it through that.*

Keep going—your future self will thank you.

self-help resources

FIND MENTAL HEALTH CARE

Psychology Today
https://www.psychologytoday.com

GoodTherapy
https://www.goodtherapy.org

NeedyMeds
https://www.needymeds.org/free-clinics

Open Path Psychotherapy Collective
https://openpathcollective.org

Alma
https://helloalma.com

Inclusive Therapists
https://www.inclusivetherapists.com

MENTAL HEALTH ORGANIZATIONS

National Suicide Prevention Lifeline
https://suicidepreventionlifeline.org
800-273-8255

Crisis Text Line
https://www.crisistextline.org
Text HOME to 741741

RAINN (Rape, Abuse & Incest National Network)
https://www.rainn.org
Hotline: 800-656-4673

SAMHSA (Substance Abuse and Mental Health Services Administration)
https://www.samhsa.gov
Helpline: 800-662-4357

The Trevor Project
https://www.thetrevorproject.org
866-488-7386

FOR MORE READING

Atlas of the Heart: Mapping Meaningful Connection and the Language of Human Experience by Brené Brown

It Didn't Start with You: How Inherited Family Trauma Shapes Who We Are and How to End the Cycle by Mark Wolynn

The Unspeakable Mind: Stories of Trauma and Healing from the Frontlines of PTSD Science by Shaili Jain, M.D.

What Happened to You?: Conversations on Trauma, Resilience, and Healing by Bruce D. Perry, M.D., Ph.D. and Oprah Winfrey

Why We Sleep: Unlocking the Power of Sleep and Dreams by Matthew Walker, Ph.D.

references

American Psychological Association. "Trauma." *APA*. https://www.apa.org/topics/trauma.

Anchor, Shawn. *The Happiness Advantage: How a Positive Brain Fuels Success in Work and Life*. New York, NY: Currency, 2010.

Jain, Shaili. *The Unspeakable Mind: Stories of Trauma and Healing from the Frontlines of PTSD Science*. New York, NY: Harper, 2019.

Newhouse, Leo. "Is Crying Good for You?" *Harvard Health Publishing*, 2021. https://www.health.harvard.edu/blog/is-crying-good-for-you-2021030122020.

Perry, Bruce D. and Winfrey, Oprah. *What Happened to You?: Conversations on Trauma, Resilience, and Healing*. New York, NY: Flatiron Books, 2021.

Van der Kolk, Bessel. *The Body Keeps the Score: Brain, Mind, and Body in the Healing of Trauma*. New York, NY: Penguin Books, 2015.

Wolynn, Mark. *It Didn't Start with You: How Inherited Family Trauma Shapes Who We Are and How to End the Cycle*. New York, NY: Penguin Books, 2017.

Yan, Holly. "The National Sexual Assault Hotline got a 201% increase in calls during the Kavanaugh hearing." *CNN*, 2018. https://www.cnn.com/2018/09/24/health/national-sexual-assault-hotline-spike/index.html.

acknowledgments

Like healing, writing this book was a long and challenging process that brought out big feelings and, at times, left me crumpled on the floor—and it's a journey I couldn't have done alone.

Mom, thank you for revisiting your traumatic past and discussing my childhood with me. I know it wasn't easy.

Andrea, thank you for allowing me to share a piece of your story and for your support and encouragement these past several years. You're an inspiration.

My agent, Michele: thank you for securing the book deal of my dreams and advocating for me throughout the process.

My editor, Melody, and the Hay House team: thank you for believing in my vision and voice. I'm so grateful for all the work you've done to bring this book to life. I couldn't have asked for a better publishing partner.

My friends and family who've cheered me on throughout this journey: thank you so much. Shout-out to Valerie, Brian, Kendall, and Angela for celebrating my wins with me, making them feel extra special.

Thank you to my therapists for holding space for my pain and helping me along my healing journey. I'm so grateful for all you've taught me.

Krissa, thank you for helping me become a better writer.

Julia, thank you for lightening my load and taking work off my plate, so I had the time and space to write this book.

My sweet pup, Sammy: your unconditional love has helped me through some dark times, and I'm so lucky to have you. I rescued you, but there have been days where you've rescued me too.

Adam, thank you for supporting my healing and my dreams and for believing in me when it felt like nobody else did.

Finally, my deepest gratitude to the @HealingFromPTSD community. Thank you for sharing your struggles, fears, and stories with me, and for supporting my work. This book wouldn't exist without you.

about the author

Born and raised in the Bay Area, Madeline Popelka grew up in a household where mental health was never discussed. Suffering alone, when she started to experience PTSD symptoms in her late twenties, she realized she didn't know the first step in getting help.

As Madeline began her healing journey, she felt an urge to create a space for other trauma survivors on Instagram, @HealingFromPTSD, which is now the largest trauma healing community on Instagram. There she shares her hard-earned lessons on healing, inspiring hundreds of thousands of survivors along their healing journeys.

To learn more about Madeline and her work, visit her website at madelinepopelka.com and her Instagram: @HealingFromPTSD.

Hay House Titles of Related Interest

HAY HOUSE
Online Video Courses

Your journey to a better life starts with figuring out which path is best for you. Hay House Online Courses provide guidance in mental and physical health, personal finance, telling your unique story, and so much more!

LEARN HOW TO:

- choose your words and actions wisely so you can tap into life's magic

- clear the energy in yourself and your environments for improved clarity, peace, and joy

- forgive, visualize, and trust in order to create a life of authenticity and abundance

- manifest lifelong health by improving nutrition, reducing stress, improving sleep, and more

- create your own unique angelic communication toolkit to help you to receive clear messages for yourself and others

- use the creative power of the quantum realm to create health and well-being

To find the guide for your journey,
visit www.HayHouseU.com.

HAY HOUSE
online learning

CONNECT WITH
HAY HOUSE
ONLINE

🌐 hayhouse.co.uk   **f** @hayhouse

📷 @hayhouseuk   🐦 @hayhouseuk

▶️ @hayhouseuk   ♪ @hayhouseuk

'*The gateways to wisdom and knowledge are always open.*'

Louise Hay